The Cambridge Introduction to
T. S. Eliot

T. S. Eliot was not only one of the most important poets of the twentieth century; as literary critic and commentator on culture and society, his writing continues to be profoundly influential. Every student of English must engage with his writing to understand the course of modern literature. This book provides the perfect introduction to key aspects of Eliot's life and work, as well as to the wider contexts of modernism in which he wrote. John Xiros Cooper explains how Eliot was influenced by the intellectual climate of both twentieth-century Britain and America, and how he became a major cultural figure on both sides of the Atlantic. The continuing controversies surrounding his writing and his thought are also addressed. With a useful guide to further reading, this is the most informative and accessible introduction to T. S. Eliot.

JOHN XIROS COOPER is Professor of English and Associate Dean in the Faculty of Arts at the University of British Columbia, Vancouver.

Cambridge Introductions to Literature

This series is designed to introduce students to key topics and authors. Accessible and lively, these introductions will also appeal to readers who want to broaden their understanding of the books and authors they enjoy.

- Ideal for students, teachers, and lecturers
- Concise, yet packed with essential information
- Key suggestions for further reading

Titles in this series:

Bulson *The Cambridge Introduction to James Joyce*

Cooper *The Cambridge Introduction to T. S. Eliot*

Dillon *The Cambridge Introduction to Early English Theatre*

Goldman *The Cambridge Introduction to Virginia Woolf*

Holdeman *The Cambridge Introduction to W. B. Yeats*

McDonald *The Cambridge Introduction to Samuel Beckett*

Peters *The Cambridge Introduction to Joseph Conrad*

Scofield *The Cambridge Introduction to the American Short Story*

Thomson *The Cambridge Introduction to English Theatre, 1600–1900*

Todd *The Cambridge Introduction to Jane Austen*

The Cambridge Introduction to
T. S. Eliot

JOHN XIROS COOPER

CAMBRIDGE
UNIVERSITY PRESS

CAMBRIDGE UNIVERSITY PRESS
Cambridge, New York, Melbourne, Madrid, Cape Town, Singapore, São Paulo

CAMBRIDGE UNIVERSITY PRESS
The Edinburgh Building, Cambridge CB2 2RU, UK

Published in the United States of America by Cambridge University Press, New York

www.cambridge.org
Information on this title: www.cambridge.org/9780521547598

First published 2006

Printed in the United Kingdom at the University Press, Cambridge

A catalogue record for this book is available from the British Library

ISBN-13 978-0-521-83888-7 hardback
ISBN-10 0-521-83888-6 hardback
ISBN-13 978-0-521-54759-8 paperback
ISBN-10 0-521-54759-8 paperback

For Kelly

Contents

viii   *Contents*

Preface

Walk into any university or college library, look up T. S. Eliot in the catalogue, and you will be confronted with many shelves and banks of books by and about him. Most of the books about Eliot, however, are scholarly studies looking at specific aspects of his work. Many of these are written for specialists. This *Introduction*, on the other hand, is written for readers who are, perhaps, new to Eliot but would like an overview of the life and work in order to know more about the man and understand something about his poetry, his ideas, and his place in twentieth-century literary history.

There is as much interest in Eliot now as at any time in the past seventy or eighty years, yet what today's community of readers and critics has to say about him reflects current issues and concerns. Past introductions and companions have helped readers in previous generations to come to grips with a poet whose work can be difficult, but from perspectives that are grounded in their time. This book owes a great debt to those earlier scholars and critics who have contributed so much to our knowledge of the poet. We can say of our understanding of this wealth of scholarship and commentary what Eliot said about a poet's relationship to the writers of the past. We know more than they do, but they are what we know. This *Introduction* rests on the work of those who have thought and written about Eliot over the years. Some distinguished literary critics have in fact themselves offered introductory commentaries. George Williamson's *A Reader's Guide to T. S. Eliot* (1953) still has much to offer in the way of particular analyses of the key poems. Northrop Frye's small book on the poet, *T. S. Eliot* (1963), provides a compelling, but acerbic, reading of Eliot's ideas. Perhaps the most popular short introduction for students has been B. C. Southam's *A Student's Guide to the Selected Poems of T. S. Eliot* (1969) and it is still a very useful guide. There are also a number of casebooks and A. D. Moody's essential *The Cambridge Companion to T. S. Eliot* (1994) for those who would like to pursue the work in more detail.

The current book has been written to introduce a great poet to a new generation of readers, students as well as the general reader. It tries to capture the complexity of a difficult man and poet but in a language and approach that will not alienate the nonspecialist. An introduction, however, is no substitute for direct knowledge of the work. If you are encouraged by what you read here to acquaint yourself more fully with T. S. Eliot, then this little book will have achieved its primary goal.

Abbreviations

ASG	*After Strange Gods: A Primer of Modern Heresy.* London: Faber and Faber, 1934
CP	*Collected Poems: 1909–1962.* London: Faber and Faber, 1968
FLA	*For Lancelot Andrewes: Essays on Style and Order.* London: Faber and Faber, 1928
Idea	*The Idea of a Christian Society.* London: Faber and Faber, 1939
Notes	*Notes Towards the Definition of Culture.* 1948; rpt. London: Faber and Faber, 1988
PP	*On Poetry and Poets.* London: Faber and Faber, 1957
SE	*Selected Essays.* 1932; rpt. London: Faber and Faber, 1951
SW	*The Sacred Wood: Essays on Poetry and Criticism.* 1919; rpt. London: Methuen, 1957
Use	*The Use of Poetry and the Use of Criticism.* 1933; rpt. London: Faber and Faber, 1964

Chapter 1

Life

Early life, 1888–1914

At East Coker in the English county of Somerset, St. Michael's parish church, situated on gently rising ground, looks out over a benign setting of trees, fields, and a scattering of ancient-seeming cottage roofs. On a warm, sunny day in late summer, it is easy to imagine oneself standing before a landscape unchanged for centuries. Only the presence of one or two cars in the church carpark and the encroachments of a new housing estate just visible in the far distance remind travelers that they are still very much in the twenty-first century. Inside, stained-glass illuminates, here and there, the dark interior. At the back, in the right-hand corner, a modest memorial marks the place in the wall where T. S. Eliot's ashes are interred. The poet himself chose this place for the deposition of his remains. The choice is significant. Here in this modest, virtually anonymous place, he enjoys eternity in an old village off the main track, in a church difficult to find, and in a place where no public sign or fanfare trumpets the presence of a celebrated author. Only when you enter the church do you know that you have arrived.

A visitor without any knowledge of the literary culture of the twentieth century might be excused for thinking that the "Thomas Stearns Eliot, Poet" remembered in St. Michael's was a minor figure, of limited importance, memorialized by an obscure parish in a small, out of the way village only for want of more famous native sons. But the visitor would be quite wrong. The obscurity of the resting place contrasts with the fame and celebrity of the man. That Eliot preferred this place as opposed to the thrust of a louder monument reveals an essential quality of the man's character. But if one therefore believed that the meaning of this resting place shows us the modesty and, even, humility of the man, this, too, would be wide of the mark. The simplicity of the ending at East Coker contrasts with a complex life and, equally, a tangle of motivations even in the simple matter of laying one's remains to rest. The symbolism of the ending in Somerset reflects the intricacies of a life that was neither simple nor straightforward, nor even modest or humble, though modesty and humility are an essential part of the story. The first complication stems from the fact that Eliot was not a native of Somerset at all. He was born on September 26, 1888 in St. Louis, Missouri on the banks of the Mississippi River in late nineteenth-century America. East Coker was primarily an imaginary origin; a genealogical fact, to be sure, but not, for all that, any the less a self-defining fiction.

Eliot was born into a prominent family with roots in Boston and the New England of the early pilgrims. His ancestors had left Somerset in the 1650s and made their way across the Atlantic to the Massachusetts colony where, over time, they established themselves as social and cultural leaders. In St. Louis the family tradition held firm and Eliot was raised to see his destiny in terms of a life dedicated to the highest cultural ideals, manifested in an ethic of service through established social and cultural institutions. Throughout his life, Eliot never lost this sense of purpose. It perhaps explains his lifelong defence of tradition and the institutions, such as the Church, a blood aristocracy, and, of course, education, that sustain it.

When Eliot was seven he began his formal education, first attending a small elementary school operated by a Mrs. Lockwood, and then, in autumn 1898, entering Smith Academy in order to prepare for university study. In St. Louis Smith was considered an educational stepping stone to the best universities. Eliot read widely as a boy and devoted himself to schoolwork; indeed, he became a model student.

In 1905, on completing the course of studies at Smith, Eliot was destined for Harvard University and to prepare for this he was enrolled at Milton Academy, a private school near Boston, which sent many young men to Harvard. This was his first experience of being away from home for an extended period. He completed his year at Milton successfully and headed for Harvard in 1906. He excelled in this new environment and would remain there until 1914, pursuing a masters degree and doctorate. His intellectual and literary activities set him apart again, but this time in ways that were more productive. Harvard, at this time, along with other Ivy League schools, was filled with the sons of rich and powerful families and Eliot found himself in the company of many young men whose interests and life choices were rarely intellectual or literary. For most of the other students, Harvard was a youthful deferral of their espousal of the family business, a career in politics, or a life of conspicuous leisure. Yet although Eliot's scholarly pursuits and his growing intellectual vigor set him apart from the somewhat lazy and undisciplined behavior of many of his fellow students, he was not entirely alienated from their easy and uncomplicated world. He belonged to the right student clubs and societies and participated in the quotidian activities of most other students. There was no hint yet of the bohemian poet. But Harvard was more than a social club; it was also a place of learning and of serious work and, Eliot took to that side of university life like a duck to water. In keeping with the American system of undergraduate education, he read and studied widely in several different disciplines. Being a bit of a dud in sciences, he was drawn to the traditional humanities, studying the literatures of several countries, languages, history, and philosophy.

In 1910 Eliot underwent the American version of that old British coming-of-age tradition, the Grand Tour. Unlike the Grand Tour, however, the Junior Year Abroad is not a tour of Europe – primarily of France and Italy, and occasionally Greece – on which the sons of aristocrats in the eighteenth and nineteenth centuries whiled away a few months among ruins and classical buildings before settling down on the family estate to while away the years making life miserable for foxes, portrait painters, wives, and, in many cases, tenant farmers. Whether the sons picked up any wisps of culture or learning on their travels was at the end of the day neither here nor there. Indeed, these richly leisured tourists usually picked up nothing more than syphilis for their troubles. The American Junior Year Abroad is a different kind of ceremonial. First of all, it needs to be earnestly educational. The idea of basking in the Roman Forum among the weeds, the broken stones, and the staring lizards simply to soak up some culture has never sat well with the American temperament. Purposeless meandering is not part of the itinerary of success. The intention of the Junior Year Abroad may be similar to the Grand Tour, that is, to give the young person an expansive cultural experience of the European inheritance, but it must be organized, certified, and on schedule.

Eliot's year abroad from Harvard was not actually a tour as such; it was mainly limited to Paris, with excursions to London and Munich, but more importantly it was a year of serious study. In September 1910 he set out from America for the Sorbonne to study French literature, which in his case meant, among many authors, a steady and concentrated reading of Charles Baudelaire, Jules Laforgue, and Tristan Corbière, to all of whom Arthur Symons in a little book on French poetry had given Eliot an introduction.[1] Like many other students and people of fashion in Paris, he also attended the lectures of the preeminent French philosopher of his day, Henri Bergson, at the Collège de France. He took French conversation lessons from Alain-Fournier, the author of a magical work of fiction called *Le Grande Meaulnes* (1913), a novel that evokes with dreamy lyricism an idyllic France. He made a close friend of another young Frenchman, a medical student named Jean Verdenal who lived in the same student *pension* as Eliot. Both these friends died in the First World War. Verdenal's death was a particularly heavy blow, and Eliot's homage to his friend was expressed in the dedication of his first book of poetry in 1917.

On his return to Boston in 1911, Eliot finished his first degree and moved on to a masters. He now seemed headed for an academic career as a philosopher, much to the delight of his father and family in general. Privately he was writing verses – mainly in fragments – while he concentrated on philosophy. It was during his M.A. studies that he attended a seminar by the British philosopher Bertrand Russell. Russell had come to Harvard as a visiting professor in 1914 and Eliot impressed him enough as a student for the famous philosopher to mention him in a letter to one of his closest English friends, Lady Ottoline Morrell, who was, in turn, to figure large in Eliot's life as well when he arrived in England in the late summer of 1914. In that letter Russell recorded being struck by Eliot's intellectual strengths and his taste, but he felt that Eliot was "ultra-civilized" and lacking in "vigour or life – or enthusiasm."[2] By that time Eliot was already looking ahead to doctoral work and a period of philosophical travel in Europe was already in the works. Russell, knowing that Oxford University was one of the stops on this intellectual itinerary, thought him well suited emotionally to that ancient seat of learning.

In the summer of 1914, bearing his new M.A. degree and with doctoral work ahead, Eliot took up a Sheldon Traveling Fellowship for a year's study at Merton College, Oxford, with Harold Joachim, the preeminent interpreter of F. H. Bradley's philosophical work, about which Eliot was to write his doctoral thesis. But before arriving at Oxford, he alighted in Europe early in the summer for some touring. This was part two of the Junior Year Abroad, and again education was as important as simple sightseeing. He was enrolled on a summer program of study at Marburg University in Germany, but on his way to Marburg he stopped in Belgium and Italy, visiting galleries and other tourist sights. He looked at paintings, visited monuments, and was mildly admiring of castles, chateaux, and stately homes.

By mid-July he had arrived in Marburg and was just settling into his course of study when the political crisis that would lead to the First World War made a German sojourn no longer possible. As war clouds gathered he deserted Marburg and arrived in London just as the ultimatums mounting among the

Western powers spilled over into declarations of war. Eliot took rooms in Bloomsbury and began to make the acquaintance of other writers and poets. Conrad Aiken, a Harvard friend and aspiring writer, had been in London the year before and had spoken to a number of people about Eliot; indeed, he had shown an early version of his poem "The Love Song of J. Alfred Prufrock" to Harold Munro, the proprietor of the Poetry Bookshop, who had judged the poem "absolutely insane."[3] More productively, Aiken had shown the poem to another expatriate American living in London, Ezra Pound, and had received a quite different assessment. He had therefore written to Eliot urging him to contact Pound while he was in London before going down to Oxford for the autumn term in October.

This was the year in which Eliot met a young woman, Vivien Haigh-Wood, who visited Oxford occasionally to see friends there. Much to the dismay of their families, they married after a whirlwind three-month courtship. The man responsible for introducing them was another American studying at Oxford, Scofield Thayer. Eliot had known him at Milton Academy and Harvard and Thayer would later play an important role in the early 1920s in bringing to the light of day Eliot's first great poem, *The Waste Land* (1922). It appears, that Vivien was Eliot's first experience of intimacy with a woman. At first he was attracted by her youthful vivacity but later, when the extent of her ill health became evident, his relationship to her changed dramatically.

A bohemian life, 1915–1922

Eliot and Vivien were an odd couple from the start. The quiet, studious, highly self-conscious philosopher-poet with impeccable manners found himself in the constant company of a chirpy, nervous woman suffering from both physical and psychological ailments. When well, she was animated and lively, with a taste for night life, the theater, dancing, and dining out. When ill, she was sunk in a sodden depression. For a time Eliot tried to keep up with her, but it was a losing battle and he became increasingly conscious of his inadequacy. Indeed, he may have contributed to her depression, as he grew more remote and reserved; cold and distant might be another way of putting it. As a result, she sought solace in the company of others. It is difficult to know what kind of sexual relationship they had, but it could not have been a satisfying one. It is clear now that after a time, with her marriage sinking into desuetude, Vivien entered into a sexual relationship with Russell. It is not clear whether Eliot was dismayed by this or relieved. It was probably a bit of both. Her health deteriorated in the years after their marriage and she soon became a somewhat pathetic creature, having to endure the sympathy of her own friends and, worse, of her husband's friends and colleagues.

There has always been rumor and speculation about Eliot's influence on his wife's health, especially her mental equilibrium. It has been said, and recently repeated in a biography of Vivien,[4] that Eliot's emotional apathy, his coldness of affection or lack of feeling, undermined her sense of wellbeing and, in daily increments of disaffection, drove her mad. Without a doubt, Eliot was not an emotionally demonstrative person and this has sometimes been interpreted as a debilitating remoteness that shut his wife, and others, out of his inner life. Yet it cannot be said that Eliot was without emotions; he was a man of profound feeling and, in many respects, a man of passion. He was also highly concerned about his wife's ill health on a day-to-day basis. He stood by her in those early years of the marriage and served her devotedly. Indeed, it is a matter of record among his friends and acquaintances at the time that he went far beyond what was required in helping Vivien to cope with her ailments. He sacrificed a good deal of his time to taking care of her needs, time that he could have devoted to his writing. In this he was unselfish, and not just in this special instance of husbandly responsibility. He was not a selfish man, and although not generous in sharing his feelings with others, he was generous in many other ways.

The difficulties of the marriage were not restricted to the physical and emotional health of the couple. The Eliots, now living in London, were also constantly in need of money. They were not poor, but making ends meet during the First World War proved a full-time occupation. Russell, a man of means, helped a little with funds, and some money came from America, but not enough. Eliot was put in the position of having to earn his living, and he turned to teaching and lecturing. He was not happy in these occupations and, although he did an adequate job, not particularly successful. He was not a natural teacher for whom personal magnetism might compensate for a certain weakness of pedagogical technique. It seems he had little of either. He was, in the essentials of human intercourse, an invisible man, always having to be in character, as if he were wearing a mask. Perhaps it was temperamental, perhaps a species of protective covering for a shy, self-conscious, despairing man. This doubleness of personality, commented on by many who knew him, would become in later years a source of profound consternation for friends.

In addition to teaching, Eliot took to book reviewing as a way of supplementing his income. At this he was far more successful than he was at teaching, not in terms of income but in terms of experience. He reviewed for a number of journals but principally for the *Times Literary Supplement* and, through Russell's good offices, the *International Journal of Ethics* and the *New Statesman.* Some of his most important critical and literary historical formulations, later developed into essays of great consequence, were first adumbrated in these periodicals. The reviewing business had a number of other beneficial effects. For one thing, he had the opportunity to read widely in a number of fields and to keep abreast of developments in philosophy and adjacent disciplines after his professional interest in philosophy began to decline. Reviewing also clarified his writing style, stripping from it the remaining mannerisms of the academy. Literary journalism gave him an opportunity to talk directly to other writers, editors, and critics of London's literary scene. Unlike the cloistered virtues of scholarship, the literary review thrust Eliot into the commotion of public debate. On this new terrain he honed a polemical style of great power and authority. Apart from his subsequent influence as a literary critic and theorist, his refinement of several writerly virtues – clarity, concision, concreteness – made him, in addition to his poetry, one of the great prose stylists of the twentieth century.

Teaching could provide sufficient income to survive, but it required a greater personal commitment and level of energy than Eliot was able to give it. He did owe teaching one important influence on his prose style, however. In his critical writings he adopted, as a kind of satirical mask, the schoolmasterly fastidiousness in definition of terms (see the opening pages of *The Sacred Wood*, on the words "organized" and "activity"). This early concern with denotative precision was one small step in creating a professional critical persona. Slowly, the schoolmasterly manner evolved into the more serious persona of cultural sage. But that was to come much later. In order to establish a more authoritative gravity than was possible with the droll figure of the tsk-tsking schoolmaster, Eliot had to pass, somewhat improbably, through the world of banking and business. Vivien's family connections helped Eliot to find a place with Lloyds Bank in the financial heart of the British capital, the area known as the City. In March 1917 he joined the Colonial and Foreign Department and began an eight-year career in banking. It was a secure job with a good income, less taxing than teaching, and with an aura of respectability that contrasted rather unusually with Eliot's activities as a poet, especially a poet with bohemian affiliations. Within a few months of joining Lloyds, his first book of poems, *The Love Song of J. Alfred Prufrock and Other Observations*, was published by the Egoist Press, under the control of Harriet Shaw Weaver, a patron of the avant-garde arts. *Prufrock*, as one of the key books of early modernist literature, had been preceded at the press by two other modernist classics, James Joyce's *A Portrait of the Artist as a Young Man* (1916) and Wyndham Lewis's *Tarr* (1916).

Eliot's work at the bank continued to provide him with a steady income as his literary activities increased in volume and significance. He began to appear regularly in the literary periodicals and reviews. At Pound's urging he accepted an assistant editor's position with the *Egoist* magazine, and he also contributed to it. His circle of friends and colleagues in London widened and soon he was on friendly enough terms with Leonard and Virginia Woolf to have them publish under their Hogarth Press imprint his next book of poems, called simply *Poems*, in June 1919. The volume was also published in America by the most important publisher of modernist work in New York, Alfred Knopf. This volume gathered together his most recent work, including a small number of French poems that brought the influence of the *symbolistes* to fruition. The book also contained poems written in traditional quatrain stanzas, the product of experiments in verse that Eliot and Pound conducted as together they studied the prosodic sophistication of the nineteenth-century French poet Théophile Gauthier.

With the composition of "Gerontion" in the spring of 1919, Eliot entered one of his most fertile periods, culminating in the publication of his greatest early poem, *The Waste Land*. His personal life was by then a shambles, his marriage clearly a failure. Both his health and Vivien's had deteriorated. Eliot's ailments were psychological and emotional; worry and exhaustion led to bouts of depression as well as severe headaches all through 1919 and 1920, though occasional trips to France helped to invigorate him and contact with other pioneering writers of his generation, such as Lewis, Joyce, Pound, and others, afforded him the right kind of literary conversation and contacts. Yet he was never able to shake off the depression entirely. The routine life of the banker, though stable, rankled. It took up a great deal of time, time that could have been devoted to writing. For some, this emotional climate might have dried up the creative juices. Eliot did occasionally slip into arid periods, but, oddly, between 1919 and 1922 he was remarkably productive. In 1919, he composed "Gerontion" and other fragments that eventually became *The Waste Land*.

With the end of the First World War in 1918, Eliot's financial and domestic position had not changed. Worries over money, his wife's abdominal disorders, her increasingly fragile mental state, and his own feelings of nervous exhaustion fed a growing sense of despair. The immediate postwar situation in Britain and Europe added to the sense of collapse and chaos. In a letter to Richard Aldington, a writer friend, Eliot expressed fear and loathing of the contemporary social and economic scene. In this gloomy atmosphere he began work on pulling together the fragments of a long poem that he called, provisionally, "He Do the Police in Different Voices."

The title came from a phrase in one of his favourite novels, Charles Dickens's *Our Mutual Friend*, which he would use again in *Old Possum's Book of Practical Cats* (1939). He was working on the poem in late 1920 and early 1921. By February 1921 he had already shown what was then a four-part poem to friends. He was still at work on it in the summer when his mother Charlotte and sister Marian arrived from America for a visit. He had hoped to have made progress, indeed even to have finished it, by June, but the poem was proving unruly. He struggled with it into the autumn, but was still not satisfied. His life grew increasingly complicated and this interfered with the creative process.

His mother's visit was a distraction in a number of ways. His American relations were not happy with his decision to stay in England and they held Vivien partly responsible for this. The relationship between his wife and his mother was fraught with palpable dislike. There was tension also between Charlotte and some of Eliot's artistic friends and acquaintances. The sober Puritan from New England did not like the rather more colorful members of her son's acquaintance. These strains made it very clear to Eliot that he had, for good or ill, slipped out of the emotional and intellectual orbit of his family in America. Yet it was also clear to him that he had not as yet entered into a new sphere of national and cultural loyalties either. He was, as it were, a figure in exile in England, a resident alien, or to use his term for this condition, *metoikos*. This Greek word referred to residents of a Greek city, say Athens, who had the right to live and work in the city but, because they were foreigners, did not have full citizenship rights. Although Eliot would eventually integrate more fully into British life, this sense of being an outsider, a *metoikos*, never left him completely.

These domestic issues were not the only impediments to the completion of the new poem. In the summer one of Eliot's friends, Sidney Schiff, introduced him to the wife of the proprietor of a major London newspaper, the *Daily Mail*. Lady Rothermere fancied herself an important patron of the arts and was particularly interested in the founding of a literary review, among other possible ventures. She saw in Eliot a potential editor and he was interested in a venture that would give him access to a periodical. Through it he could propagate not only his ideas about literary criticism but, and perhaps, more significantly for him, his ideas about social and cultural life as well. He was still relatively young, keenly intelligent, well connected in avant-garde circles, and, from the perspective of a rich patron, a reliable man, a steady employee of Lloyds Bank. Although the conversations and negotiations with Lady Rothermere were not easy, they were concluded more or less successfully and the first number of the new review was scheduled for January 1922. In fact, it was not launched until October of that year.

As the summer of 1921 progressed, the unfinished long poem still hung over his head. As well as the domestic and literary distractions, there were important aesthetic experiences that helped to shape the work to come. One was Eliot's awareness of Joyce's *Ulysses*, which was in the process of being readied for publication that summer. Eliot knew of its content and method from personal contact with Joyce. It was the book's method that particularly caught his eye. In a subsequent review, after the novel's publication in February 1922, Eliot wrote that Joyce's greatest achievement was his use of the "mythic method," that is, the use of ancient myth as a way of looking at the present time.[5] It was a way of making sense of or bringing order to the chaos and confusion of the contemporary world. This insight had far-reaching consequences, both for our understanding of the nature and status of myth and for the evolution of a cultural conservatism that took the inherited conservatism of blood, land, and tradition to a new extreme. It was an insight that would reach its most toxic form in the myth-drenched politics of European fascism.

Myth was also at the core of Eliot's other memorable aesthetic experience in that fateful summer. He attended a performance of Igor Stravinsky's ballet *Le Sacre de Printemps* and he afterward reported that at its conclusion he was overwhelmed, so much so that he stood up and cheered. The primeval pulse, expressed in the music's rhythm and dissonance, running like an electric current through the piece, seemed to make the very same ancient connection as *Ulysses*, but in sonic terms. All the triviality, perplexity, and muddled turmoil of the modern world were for a moment swept aside by an artistic vision grounded in an ancient fertility ritual by the brusque beating of a primitive drum. This alertness to the proximity of the primitive and contemporary had its origins no doubt in his experiences of late nineteenth-century Missouri. With frontier society still within living memory, the fusion of savage and city, as Robert Crawford has suggested, provided Eliot not only with an important theme but also with a whole way of perceiving modernity.[6]

With the coming of autumn, Eliot had still not made sufficient progress on "He Do the Police in Different Voices." A very bad bout of flu had been followed in September by a series of migraine-like cluster headaches. He was physically very tired and suffering from anxiety disorders bordering on panic attacks. His doctor feared that he was heading for a nervous breakdown of some kind and advised that he take a three-month rest cure. Eliot, though reluctant at first, decided to heed this advice. The bank gave him a three-month leave of absence in October and Eliot and Vivien went to Margate on the southeast coast of England to begin a therapeutic rest period. While there Eliot continued to work on the poem and Margate as a place eventually found its way into the published poem. In the meantime, Eliot was advised by Lady Ottoline Morrell, by now a friend, to consult a specialist in nervous disorders. She herself had been seen by a doctor in Lausanne, Switzerland, a man by the name of Roger Vittoz, whom she recommended highly. Consequently, in November he returned to London and then, with Vivien, set off, first for Paris, where Vivien checked into a sanatorium for medical reasons of her own. Having taken the poem with him to Paris, Eliot left the manuscript with Pound, who was living there at the time. From Paris Eliot continued to Lausanne and began his treatment with the Swiss doctor. There he wrote, in a moment of inspiration, what became the fifth and final part of the poem.

When Eliot returned to Paris in late January 1921, he found Pound working over the manuscript of the new poem. Pound had felt his way into the interior of what Eliot had produced and by excising about half the lines was able to lift from the fragments a whole poem that he now called *The Waste Land*. Eliot agreed at once with the change of title. Part V, "What the Thunder Said," seemed to fit precisely with the movement and mood of the poem disinterred from the original draft by Pound and Pound suggested simply adding the new section as it had been composed in Lausanne without any changes. What Pound discovered in the heart of the poem was its mythic core. It was this discovery and the subsequent creative collaboration between the two Americans that helped to produce the most famous poem of the twentieth century.

Back in London, with *The Waste Land* in hand, Eliot finally concluded the negotiations with Lady Rothermere and brought his new review, the *Criterion*, to life. In October 1922, in the very first number, Eliot launched his new poem. It was also published a month later in America in Scofield Thayer's literary magazine, the *Dial*, after some rather ill-tempered negotiations. Thayer arranged to give Eliot, as part-payment, the *Dial* poetry prize of two thousand dollars that year. In addition, Thayer was obliged to take 350 copies of the first American book publication of *The Waste Land*. The firm owned by Horace Liveright brought out the poem in December 1922. All these American negotiations and contractual agreements were arranged by a New York lawyer named John Quinn, to whom many of the avant-garde writers of the time owed much in terms of advice in legal and commercial transactions. In order to thank Quinn, Eliot gave him the manuscript of the original poem, with Pound's editorial comments. At this point, the manuscript dropped from view and it was not rediscovered until the late 1960s after Eliot's death. In England the book publication of the poem came almost a year later, in September 1923, from the Hogarth Press, still being operated by the Woolfs in their house. By that time the poem had already had an enormous impact. Along with Joyce's *Ulysses*, it helped to define in the public's mind the character of the modern movement in literature.

Man of letters, 1923–1945

Eliot's new position as editor of the *Criterion* gave him a podium on which he was able to enlarge his profile. As a result of the new income provided by Lady Rothermere, he was finally able to put Lloyd's Bank behind him. Not that he disliked what was in effect his day job; he often expressed his gratitude to the bank for giving him economic, and some personal, stability. But it was time-consuming and tedious work, nevertheless, and after eight years in the City, Eliot was glad to bring his employment there to an end. For two years he struggled with the *Criterion*, never achieving the independence and control that he felt he needed to realize his plans for the review. He was grateful to Lady Rothermere and her money, but she did not make life easy. Her commitment to the enterprise wavered and, finally, in 1925, collapsed. Eliot reduced the publication schedule in order to deal with the financial crisis in which he suddenly found himself. He needed a new patron and, luckily, one came along just in time to save the enterprise. Geoffrey Faber, a fellow of All Souls College, Oxford, and a man with a family fortune behind him, had recently invested in a publishing enterprise operated by Richard Gwyer. The new firm of Faber and Gwyer (Faber and Faber from 1929) was looking for opportunities to explore new publishing directions. A fellow Soul, Charles Whibley, brought Eliot to Faber's notice and at their first meeting the two men immediately connected with each other, beginning a friendship that would last for four decades. From his position as literature editor in the new company, Eliot was able to commission and publish books by members of the new generation that was beginning to redefine British literature in the twentieth century. He also found a new home for the *Criterion*, allowing it to flourish over the next two decades. He brought new writers to the firm and aggressively recruited authors from other publishers. In fact, Eliot and the rest of the Faber brains trust were so effective in attracting new writing of the highest quality that the firm soon became the gold standard of literary excellence in modern Britain, and it remains so to this day. Indeed, one might argue that the firm defined the way in which modernity and ideas of the modern were understood in England in the twentieth century.

Also significant was the long and continuous deterioration of his marriage to Vivien. By the mid-1920s she was already manifesting the erratic and nervous behavior that would eventually lead to her institutionalization in the 1930s. In the summer of 1926, she was moving from one continental sanatorium to another, sometimes alone, sometimes with Eliot. Physically she had become a wan wraith; psychologically she was a wounded creature, often confiding her chronic anxieties and unhappiness to friends. The powerful drugs and other medications she was taking contributed to her emotional and physical distress. Eliot remained loyal to her throughout this decline in her condition, but only as a caregiver. He no longer felt the emotional attachment of a loving husband, companion, or friend. What he did, he did out of a sense of duty. In some ways, he treated her as if she were an injured extremity. One took care of it with a bandage and a sling, but one went on with life anyway, ignoring the damaged limb as much as possible. By June 1927 the marriage was dead. The couple were still together and even ventured out in public now and then, but the emotional bond that ought to define the married state was broken. It was in the midst of these personal circumstances that Eliot, much to the surprise of his friends, moved closer to the Church of England, abandoning the lukewarm Unitarianism of his youth.

The principal figures in smoothing the way for his conversion were, oddly in this very British context, two Americans, William Force Stead, Anglican chaplain of Worcester College, Oxford, and the Princeton University scholar Paul Elmer More. Perhaps as Americans they were in a better position to understand the source and scope of Eliot's needs. Stead mentored his progress toward the Church, guiding him into that part of the Anglican community known as Anglo-Catholicism. More provided intellectual stimulation and support. There were rumors at the time that Eliot might go all the way to Rome, but this was never a serious alternative. Eliot was not only entering a Church, submitting to a new spiritual discipline; he was also immersing himself, more generally, in a new way of life and this was comprehensively British. No doubt Roman Catholicism was a part of English life as well, but it was, in England at least, a faith on the margins, identified in the public mind with Ireland, republicanism, and allegiance to foreign power. The Marian persecutions of the mid-sixteenth century had created a hatred of Roman Catholics that had lasted into the twentieth century. Eliot did not hate Catholics, but he was no longer interested in remaining an outsider in his adopted land. It was Stead's opinion that Eliot's spiritual translation was akin to the return of a man to an ancestral home after a long exile and that allegiance to the Established Church, rather than a minority faith, was an essential element in a wider homecoming. It was also in some sense the return of a prodigal son, not in personal terms, but as a rejection of the reckless rupture in the fabric of seventeenth-century English society that had taken the Puritans, including Eliot's ancestors, to Massachusetts. He had already based one of his most important literary historical insights on the idea of a fundamental dissociation of sensibility in seventeenth-century English culture. That dissociation, he believed, was not simply a matter of poetic sensibility; it had political and social ramifications as well. His fierce need for a personal faith took shelter within an equally powerful social and cultural necessity. The rootless cosmopolitan in search of personal salvation had also found his way home. It was not surprising, then, that, within a few months of being confirmed in the Church of England, he also took on British nationality.

By 1930 the Eliots' marriage was in its final death throes. Vivien was desperately unhappy, complaining to friends about the horror into which they had plunged. At times their relationship seemed pervaded by little more than hatred for each other. As Vivien's physical and mental health deteriorated, Eliot seemed to grow more coldly composed and remote. But one suspects that his composure was not so sound. It was compounded from complex psychological and emotional materials. His constant swerving into states of abjection was masked by his habits of performance, an innate sense of the dramatic. Not in a gregarious or exhibitionist sense, but in the subtly droll recital of the observed behaviors of others. He could, when he wanted (and were such a thing even possible), be more English than the English. His remoteness was achieved by the resurrection in the twentieth century of a seventeenth-century intellectual custom, namely, that state of amused and clever disdain that he knew as metaphysical wit. It was protective coloring for a wounded man who had been run to ground by a dread of emotional attachments, by squeamishness about the raw meat of life, and by a mad wife.

By 1932 Eliot had had enough of the marriage and when his alma mater, Harvard University, offered him an opportunity to lecture as Charles Eliot Norton Professor in the winter of 1932–33, he not only leaped at the chance to get away for nearly a year, but conspired to make the separation from Vivien permanent. When he departed from Southampton for America on September 17, 1932, he knew that his marriage was at an end, even though he had not had the courage to tell Vivien. No doubt she suspected as much and this final blow incapacitated her. From that point on she was in steady decline until some years later her family, in the person of her brother Maurice Haigh-Wood, with Eliot's permission, committed her to an institution where, receiving the care she needed, her condition stabilized.

Seventeen years had passed since Eliot's last trip "home." Yet he was not home. Home now was England and he was soon homesick for his adopted land. In letters to friends across the Atlantic he spoke of his sense of disquiet at being back in America and, particularly, in the claustrophobic atmosphere of Boston and Cambridge. His sense of unease was exacerbated by his decision to leave Vivien for good. She was not yet aware of what awaited her on his return, and with this weighing on his mind, he threw himself into the work for which he had been engaged by Harvard. The lectures that he delivered eventually became one of his most important critical works, *The Use of Poetry and the Use of Criticism*, published in late 1933. His second lecturing engagement in America, though seemingly secondary at the time, has grown in importance over the years and still reverberates today, as we shall see in chapter 3.

After a successful year in America, Eliot returned to Britain in June 1933. He was immediately concerned with the problem of Vivien in Clarence Gate Gardens. Before returning, Eliot had instructed his lawyers in London to prepare a Deed of Separation. With the document he enclosed a private letter to Vivien explaining his actions. These two items were to be conveyed to Clarence Gate. They were delivered to her in July 1933. When he did not return to their flat from America, Vivien became hysterical. Things did not improve. The separation proved to be catastrophic for her and eventually led to a complete breakdown. Eliot felt the pain of her distress and would have preferred a more amicable separation but this was not possible in the circumstances. With Vivien's brother Maurice, Eliot helped to supervise his wife's affairs at a distance. They were never to see each other again.

Once the initial steps had been taken, Eliot felt as if a great burden had been lifted from his shoulders and years later he remembered the summer and autumn of 1933 as one of the happiest periods of his life. With the purging of Vivien from his life, Eliot's whole demeanor changed. Abjection was replaced by a kind of muted exuberance (if such a thing is possible). He was freer in the mid-1930s than at any time in his life. Even as a young university student he had been bound by conventions and habits of behavior that made life a minefield of restrictions and no-go areas. Only in the winter that he spent in Paris in 1910–11 had he had the same kind of freedom to pursue his impulses and desires. After 1933, he did not exactly strike out for radical new experiential territories, but he was able to devote his undivided attention to his work and his interests. He was alone and at the age of forty-five (and for the first time) he was completely in control of his destiny.

This could mean a number of things but for Eliot it meant freedom to pursue the solitary intimacies of private devotion and, at the same time, throw himself into the external world as a successful publisher, man of letters, and public intellectual. His sister Ada was concerned about this new state of affairs because she feared that it might stimulate in her brother dangerous tendencies, namely provoke his two great talents, "dramatism" for the outside world and "mysticism" for the interior.[7] But these were no longer two separate categories of being for her brother. They had been kept artificially apart during the Vivien years. His wife's proximity had meant for Eliot a constant need to cloak his innermost thoughts and feelings behind a veil of dramatized gestures signifying self-possession and assurance. It was a show for her eyes alone and she was a tough crowd to please. Without her constant watchfulness, the dramatic and mystical, whether this was good for him or not, came finally to form a unified whole. The mystique of performance merged seamlessly with the drama of the mystical. Perhaps the figure who best embodies this unique amalgamation is Thomas à Becket as we find him in Eliot's first important, and very successful, play, *Murder in the Cathedral* (1935). Charlotte Eliot's Victorian obsession with prophets and visionaries had found in her son a concrete embodiment in the Becket character.

It was in this period that Eliot's creative work shifted significantly from poetry to drama. He had been interested in drama from his first introduction to the Elizabethan dramatists, but he had only explored their work critically. After 1933, he began to think in terms of a practitioner. He had tried his hand at verse drama with *Sweeney Agonistes* in the 1920s, post-*Waste Land* period but had become tangled up in generic and thematic issues that he could not resolve. This was principally because he had no sturdy story to tell, only an assemblage of music hall turns, allegorical figures, and jazz syncopations that led nowhere. With Becket he had a strong character, a strong narrative, and an important personal theme. The play was written from the very heart of his new unity of being compounded from drama and mysticism. It was a turning point, perhaps the real turning point in his life, as opposed to the more conventional life crises that we normally think make for the greatest change – marriages, voyages, and conversions. At this juncture of his life, it would not be right to say that anything was possible, but much was now within reach that could not have been reached before. The name of that "much" was Emily Hale.

With one woman out of his life, another one soon took her place. She was both an old friend and a new intimate. Eliot had known Emily Hale as a young university student in Boston. After his departure for Europe in 1914, she had gone on to complete a degree in drama and then went to California to teach at Pomona College in Pasadena. Eventually she returned to New England to teach at Smith College in Amherst, Massachusetts. While in teaching at Harvard in 1932, Eliot had resumed their acquaintanceship, which had not entirely died out. Vivien's withdrawal into the shadows had given the renewed friendship the stimulus it needed. In 1934 Emily made the first of a series of visits to England to be with Eliot, visits that would not end until the late 1940s. While Vivien was alive Eliot had no intention of going through a divorce in order to make way for remarriage with Emily, and she understood Eliot's scruples on this point. The Church deplored divorce and he would not cut his faith to fit the push of mere desire. On this Eliot insisted and Emily agreed.

Whether she was happy with this arrangement we cannot really know at this remove. Her letters betray no irritation with Eliot's conscience. What could she do? It is clear that she loved him and that a sentiment of a similar kind was returned. But this kind of lop-sided exchange of affections was not the strongest ground for an adult intimacy. Indeed, it was rather infantile and completely unbalanced in favor of the stronger partner, the man. It made it easier for Eliot to embrace the idea of a relationship when she was ten thousand miles away and would come only for short visits in the summer. It also made it easier that she made no demands on him of any kind. After all, by the mid-1930s he was a celebrated author and she merely an obscure drama teacher from Pasadena and, then, Amherst, Massachusetts. So how should she presume? From Emily's behavior it seems pretty clear that she worshiped him just as he was. He worshiped her as well, but not as *she* was. He worshiped an idea of her that was the furthest possible remove from Vivien, from Vivien's hallucinations, from her dependencies, from her demands, and, above all, from her menstrual blood. Emily was ethereal, an abstraction, a fiction composed of Charlotte Eliot, the Blessed Virgin Mary, and the "hyacinth girl." It was the kind of relationship that the middle-aged man Eliot had become could eagerly embrace. Emily was unsullied, sound, and willing to perform the part she was assigned in his inner drama. Actual intimacy was not on; idealization of the woman and her remoteness from the messy physicalities of contact was the order of the day. From this protocol Eliot never wavered.

When Emily was rather badly let down in 1947, she was not reduced to hysterics like Vivien, but she was hurt nonetheless, very badly hurt. With Vivien's death in that year, Emily hurried to England believing that the last impediment to a marriage postponed for fourteen years was now gone. Eliot recoiled in horror; this was not what he had meant at all. He explained that he could not marry, as he had made a vow of celibacy that he could not break. Conjugality implied a degree of intimacy that ran against the grain of Eliot's spiritual life. The ethereal Emily was all he wanted; an Emily of flesh and blood frightened him; an Emily with claims and expectations of her own was unthinkable. The relationship struggled on after 1947 but with diminishing returns for both parties. The final blow came in 1957 when Eliot married Valerie Fletcher, his assistant of eight years at Faber and Faber. Emily was devastated by this development and never really recovered from it, though she was too well-bred to make any kind of scene.

With a more stable domestic life, Eliot was able to concentrate on his own writing with renewed vigor. The final poem in his *Collected Poems, 1909–1935* (1935), "Burnt Norton," was made from lines that he had not used in *Murder in the Cathedral*. These lines and a visit with Emily to the house at Burnt Norton near Chipping Camden in Gloucestershire combined to produce the poem that would, ten years later, open his second great long poetic sequence, *Four Quartets*. In the meantime, the success of *Murder in the Cathedral* whetted his appetite for the theater and he threw himself into writing a new play. *The Family Reunion* was staged in 1939. The Second World War interrupted his theatrical work, but Eliot turned again to drama afterward, producing three plays in eleven years: *The Cocktail Party* in 1948, *The Confidential Clerk* in 1954, and *The Elder Statesman* in 1959.

As the war approached, Eliot's work in the Church turned his attention more and more to the social and political catastrophe which was approaching in the late 1930s. By 1938, when gas masks began to be distributed to the population in England, it was very clear that the twenty-year period of peace was coming to an end. The rise of Adolf Hitler in Germany had reenergized the German state and after the Munich Crisis in November 1938 war seemed inevitable. It finally broke out in September 1939. As he carried on with his day job at Faber and Faber, Eliot began to conceive of a new work of poetry. His commitment to the theater was interrupted by the need, under conditions of total war, to close many public places, including the theaters. As a result, his creative energies returned to his first love, poetry. He realized that the poem, "Burnt Norton," that he had composed in 1935 could be extended into a suite of poems centered on various geographical locations that would act as the compass points of a whole life. "Burnt Norton" defined a moment of visionary innocence both in and out of time. "East Coker," his family's English place of origin, provided the second sacred site in this personal pilgrimage through, but ultimately beyond, self-knowledge to a wider spiritual insight. "East Coker" was written in 1940. "The Dry Salvages," in 1941, remembered his American origins both in Missouri and in New England. The final poem, "Little Gidding," composed in 1942, located the pilgrim's destination in an English religious context. The small chapel at Little Gidding brought Eliot back to the Tudor and Stuart moments in English history, defining, for Eliot, the essence of English civilization in an ambiguous historical moment, the defeat of Charles II in the Civil War of the 1640s and the continuity of spiritual life as embodied in the small but devout Anglican community of Nicholas Ferrar at Little Gidding. The visionary experience at the end of the poem recalls, but goes beyond, the visionary moment in the garden in "Burnt Norton."

Writing *Four Quartets* was only one war job of many during the war years. There were more humble tasks, at times more dangerous ones. Eliot volunteered as a fire warden during the worst of the bombing raids on London and it must have seemed the cruellest of experiences to have to watch his adopted beloved city burning from the top of the Faber building at 24 Russell Square. The solitary fire warden walking through smoldering ruins at dawn finds its way into one of the more painfully personal sections of "Little Gidding." As a man of some influence, Eliot also took it upon himself to help as many of his old and young friends as he could, recommending them for war jobs and in other ways. About Pound in Italy, broadcasting on behalf of the Italian fascists, he could do little. He did more after the war during Pound's incarceration in America as a traitor. At least he was able to keep Pound's writings in circulation during the worst of his friend's travails.

The sage, 1945–1965

By the end of the war, Eliot had achieved the position of a literary sage, the last in a long line in England stretching back to the great Victorian mentors of a nation, Thomas Carlyle, John Ruskin, George Eliot, Charles Dickens, and Matthew Arnold. With Arnold, Eliot had carried on a decades-long dialogue on the nature of poetry and culture. Many of Eliot's most significant formulations, in both literary and cultural criticism, had come as a result of that long dialogue. In 1948 his *Notes Towards the Definition of Culture* continued the conversation with Arnold, and particularly with Arnold's most significant intervention in the "culture wars" of the nineteenth century, *Culture and Anarchy* (1866). This text prodded Eliot into tackling the vexed problem of culture in a secular and materialist age. Although *Notes* was not Eliot's greatest work, the Nobel Prize jury in Stockholm felt that it was time to acknowledge Eliot's general importance and chose that year to honor him with the Nobel Prize in Literature. He was also awarded the Order of Merit by George VI in the same year. Eliot had reached the kind of success and celebrity rarely accorded a literary figure. But this image of a serenely wise man fulfilling public duties is not the whole picture. He had begun to suffer from bouts of depression from an early age and they had grown more severe in his first years in England; his first marriage had exacerbated rather than alleviated them. Even after his separation from Vivien and well into old age, these episodes continued. His religious faith had helped, but it had not entirely dispelled the affliction.

Only in relatively old age, when he was sixty-eight, did Eliot finally manage to find marital domesticity of a familiar kind. His marriage to his young assistant at Faber and Faber, Valerie Fletcher, brought a remarkable change to his life. She had been working for him from 1948 and on January 10, 1957, they were married. Eliot was suddenly content and comfortable in the intimate company of a woman who was neither frightening nor ethereal. She loved him, loved poetry, had a sense of humor, and was sensible. It was precisely what he needed. It is difficult to say what emotional nurture he gave her in return. His marriage made him, in the words of one of his biographers, "happy at last."[8] That his marriage began as an office romance probably points to the importance of Faber and Faber in Eliot's later life. Most artists avoid the kind of workaday routine which steady employment usually entails. But, as in the case of Eliot's earlier allegiance to Lloyds Bank, his commitment to Faber and Faber stabilized his life and it is perhaps not surprising in the end that it was from the ranks of colleagues that he was able to find happiness in a relationship. He was a fixture at the firm almost to the end of his life. In his seventies he reduced his work week to three days and ill-health limited his effectiveness even more. But he was a familiar presence in Russell Square even as a stooped invalid walking slowly with the help of a cane. In the 1950s he helped to bring into the Faber fold a new generation of postwar poets – Philip Larkin, Ted Hughes, and Thom Gunn, to name only three.

Eliot's vision of existence seems a recipe for paralysis rather than what might be required of an active public man. Or even of a successful private individual. Intense awareness of unattainable perfection wedded to an equally intense awareness of the unavoidable presence of oblivion does not ease the way to an active engagement with the world. Ecstasy and despair, other-worldly joy, and the horror of an existence void of meaning seemed to be the poles of his life. In between lay the wide expanse of everydayness, with its perplexities, humdrum routines, errors, squabbles, ungovernable desires, and fears. Intelligence, charm, and wit are not the personal qualities required to traverse this forlorn terrain; endurance and fortitude serve one better than misplaced hopefulness. It is difficult to say precisely when in the course of a life the defining characteristics of a person's temperament and personality are formed. In Eliot it may have been at a relatively young age. His attitude toward life was certainly not, to use an eighteenth-century epithet, an "improving" one. This contrasted starkly with the kind of optimism and sanguinity required of both the successful public personality and even more so of the successful businessperson. He was both, yet he battled depression all his life and he was prone to a punishing despair. The kind of self-confident conceit which often drives public success was undoubtedly part of the man's personality. He took pleasure in the validation of public honors, but he knew that humility was a greater virtue. Yet to some he seemed unpleasantly haughty and self-important. Even his humility was sometimes seen as a complicated kind of vanity. The glittering prizes were all his, yet in his deportment he seemed to be saying of prizes what he eventually ended up saying about poetry, that they did not matter. He was often not believed.

In his last years Eliot grew more infirm and frail, but he was in the care of his wife and she eased the pain of sickness and old age, bringing him a rare happiness even at the worst of times. Valerie was with him on the day he died of a respiratory illness on January 4, 1965. His life was richly celebrated at a memorial service in Westminster Abbey with many of his old friends, Pound for example, a legion of admirers, and public figures in attendance. It was a fittingly grand exit for the most celebrated poet of his age, who had, incongruously, become its central symbol, a curious feat for a man who all through the first six and a half decades of the twentieth century always gave the impression that he would have been more comfortable living in Elizabethan times or in *trecento* Italy. Yet there they all were in the Abbey remembering the great man. He would not have been unhappy at the attention (perhaps only because he was not there to endure it). But his approval of the grand occasion contrasts with the modesty of his choice of St. Michael's Church in Somerset as the final resting place for his ashes. This perfectly captures the clashing fractions of the man. He had become a willing monument but one hidden away in a remote part of a rural county. Only Eliot, it seems, could have found a way of bringing into alignment the public life of a great man and the hidden life of a wretched penitent. An easy man to admire, a difficult man to know.

Chapter 2

Contexts

Early influences

T. S. Eliot, as we have seen, was born on the banks of the Mississippi River in St. Louis and it is wise when considering his life and work to remember his American origins. He certainly never forgot them. He may have felt an abstract or ideal relationship to Britain and Europe, but St. Louis was, on the other hand, all too real. This was Eliot's first and most enduring context. In 1888 the city was still the gateway to the western frontier and a river city in close touch with the American South. The Civil War had not yet faded from living memory and the consequences of the South's defeat and the formal end of slavery were still very much in evidence. Although slavery had disappeared from the southern states, the systemic racism of American society as a whole, which persisted well into the twentieth century, colored every aspect of social life in St. Louis. The surrender of the South in the Civil War signified more than a political defeat; it also heralded the end of a closely knit, rural, and deeply communal society. It had been brought to its knees by the emerging industrial might of its northern adversary. Eliot's later social and cultural conservatism had its origins in the nostalgia for a South brought down by the disintegrative power of the industrial North. His yearning for a more trad-itional, hierarchical society had its beginnings in the powerful myth of community that came up the Mississippi into Missouri. Moreover, for a man destined to be one of the greatest poets of the twentieth century, his early immersion in the American language was a decisive and complicating fact in his later development. The language of America which he absorbed on the banks of the Mississippi River was infused by several conflicting discourses: the ardent idealism of America's revolutionary origins, the promise of a culture directed toward the far horizons of space and time, the heated rhetoric of populist individualism, and the many bitter legacies of African-American slavery.

His family context stimulated a love of culture at its highest levels. In counterpoint, American popular culture also exerted a powerful influence. It was when he was in his early teens that his interest in reading poetry began to manifest itself as an interest in writing it. In this he was encouraged by his mother, herself a poet with a gift of moral energy and a passionate eloquence. Her taste in poetry inclined toward the visionary and the prophetic – she was obsessed with people tingling with religious truths. Eliot's earliest enthusiasms, on the other hand, were more modest, including the ballads of Rudyard Kipling (about whom he would write a most appreciative essay later in life), Edward Fitzgerald's *The Rubáiyát of Omar Khayyám*, Byron (also the subject of a later essay), and the Elizabethan and Cavalier poets of England. A more mature study of the Elizabethans during and just after the First World War would provide Eliot with the occasion for some of his most important critical and literary historical statements. Yet his mother's habits of thought and feeling would not prove infertile. They would provide Eliot with themes of his own in the direction of religious faith. The extraordinary spiritual exertions of seers and prophets were his mother's principal poetic direction, and the figure of the saint and the martyr would appear again and again in Eliot's own work but without his mother's heated intensity, indeed in a quite different register of feeling.

France

These early influences abated when he entered Harvard as an undergraduate. His literary studies at university spanned the canon of European literature from Dante to the Elizabethan dramatists to contemporary French poetry. His reading of Charles Baudelaire was particularly important because it put him in touch with a poetic tradition in which he would find an immediate personal resonance. The French poet's synthesis of the morbid and of mordant self-scrutiny reached across the language barrier and spoke to Eliot directly. On the evidence of his later poetry and drama, Eliot was drawn to a number of things in the French poet's work: his unblinking awareness, for example, of the perpetual presence of death in the midst of life, or of the polluted materiality of the body in a culture which defines the spirit as the highest form of being. Baudelaire's strange union of narcissism and masochism must have struck a chord with Eliot, if his early poem "The Love Song of St. Sebastian" is anything to go by.[1] The young American also responded viscerally to another aspect of Baudelaire's work. European poetry up to the nineteenth century was immersed in a cultural ethos that was fundamentally rural. Even in the eighteenth century, as much of western Europe urbanized, cultural values often retained their pastoral character. The new poetry of mid-nineteenth-century France, on the other hand, located itself in the urban landscape and made the experience of the city the source of moral, spiritual, and artistic values.

Eliot's interest in French poetry grew more intense in 1908 when he picked up Arthur Symons's celebrated little book about contemporary poetry in France, *The Symbolist Movement in Literature* (1899), in the library of the Harvard Union. As Eliot admitted many years later, this little book helped to change his life.[2] In particular, Eliot was introduced for the first time to the poetry of Jules Laforgue. Even more than with Baudelaire, Eliot was fascinated by the style and mood of the younger French poet, and Laforgue triggered a sudden growth in self-awareness. It was almost as if Eliot had discovered in the Frenchman the photographic negative of his own identity. From this a positive identity would emerge, a new persona forged from all those aspects of Laforgue's personality that Symons refers to in his book: a certain provisionality of attitude and remark, fastidiousness of habit and dress, a highly evolved sense of irony, and an air of worldly fatigue. There was wit also and a certain remoteness or reserve that was to remain with Eliot for the rest of his life. It was not a passionless mask that Laforgue offered; there was definitely a kind of passion there, but it was wrapped in a curious diffidence, leaving the odd impression of infirmity.

Eliot's interest in French poetry and culture led to a year's residence in Paris. The new freedom that he felt in the French capital allowed him to indulge in desires and longings that could not have seen the light of day in Boston. He wandered the streets of less reputable *quartiers* of the city, areas frequented by prostitutes, small-time criminals, and the wretched poor. His guide book was Charles-Louis Philippe's *Bubu de Montparnasse*, a popular novel of the period which explored the seamier sides of Paris life, the sordid goings-on of prostitutes and their pimps in that defiantly bohemian *quartier* of Paris. Eliot's solitary wanderings in this nighttown of illicit desires brought him face to face with his own sexuality and lusts much as did Stephen Dedalus's sexual initiation among Dublin's prostitutes in James Joyce's *A Portrait of the Artist as a Young Man* (1916). Unlike the young Irishman, there is no evidence that Eliot did more than observe at a distance, but there is no doubt that a kind of sexual awakening occurred in those winter months walking the streets of Montparnasse. At least he was able to shrug off, for a while, the moral migraine induced by the conventional public rectitude of New England. This lightening of the moral load had its artistic consequence. He was able to complete the two most memorable poems of his early years, "Portrait of a Lady" and "The Love Song of J. Alfred Prufrock." Years later, Eliot was to remember this informal education in desire during his year abroad by recalling the novel that had given the experience its most vivid literary embodiment.

England

Eliot's fateful journey to England at the start of the First World War would provide him with the most important literary context of his life. There he came into contact with Ezra Pound. The literary and personal relationship he formed with the flamboyant Pound would last until Eliot's death in 1965. By 1914 Pound had been in London for six years and was in touch with many literary figures there. He was a gregarious and voluble man for whom networking was as natural a function as breathing. Through Pound, Eliot was quickly put in touch with his contemporaries and introduced to a vital literary scene. In late 1914 Pound was deeply involved with the movement in the visual arts called Vorticism and Eliot was introduced to the guiding intelligence of the Great London Vortex, Wyndham Lewis, with whom he remained on friendly terms for the rest of Lewis's life even when Lewis's prickly personality had made him an enemy of just about every other literary group in the British capital. Indeed, the "enemy" was one of Lewis's more endearing masquerades. Eliot was also put in touch with other expatriate American writers, H.D. (Hilda Doolittle) for one, and John Gould Fletcher. Through Pound, the ideas of the French literary critic Rémy de Gourmont and the English philosopher T. E. Hulme were also passed on.

Eliot had come to England to continue his studies at Oxford University. The university world was a familiar one and this helped Eliot to make the social and cultural transition to England. Although he did not know it in his first winter there, he would never again live in America. He would visit his home country, and spend a year there in 1932–33 as a lecturer at Harvard, but he would never again live there for any length of time. Oxford gave him a base in his new country while he sorted out what he was going to do with his life. He continued to write poetry and with the help of Pound was able to get some of it into print. In June 1915 "The Love Song of J. Alfred Prufrock" was published in Harriet Monroe's Chicago magazine, *Poetry*. In July Lewis published "Preludes" and "Rhapsody on a Windy Night" in the second, and last, number of the avant-garde magazine *Blast*. Thus 1915, the second year of the war, was the year of Eliot's arrival as a published poet.

Religion

After the publication of *The Waste Land* in 1922, Eliot's spiritual and religious life began to change, gradually at first, but a new commitment to Christianity was clear. Among his contemporaries there were doubts at first that it was genuine. The confused response to *Ash-Wednesday* in 1930 was typical. There were even suggestions, from his friend Lewis for example, that it had about it the disagreeable scent of skillful social climbing. That it was the Church of England to which he swore spiritual allegiance deepened the suspicions. After all, the Established Church in England was at the time so intricately entwined with social and political power in the country that it seemed as if Eliot, the modernist poet and bohemian artist, had simply tendered his soul to the Establishment and to mainstream society rather than to God. But appearances can be deceiving and they were in this case. Eliot's interest in religious belief and questions of faith were not of recent birth, nor were they motivated by mercenary self-interest. Undoubtedly, he was interested in the fate of his soul, but he was as equally concerned about the fate of a society moving inexorably toward thoroughgoing secularism and the materialism which accompanies it. His studies in anthropology at Harvard had already introduced him to the sociocultural importance of religion as a primordial binding force in society. A common set of transcendental beliefs made it possible for a people to experience the plenitude of a vital communal life and the psychological and emotional reassurances that come with authentic belonging.

Important as these external, intellectual factors were in directing Eliot toward a new confession of faith, his hunger for spiritual comfort in a time of personal crisis weighed heavily in the making of his decision. The anxieties and depressive episodes, a sense of sterility and spiritual sickness that led him to seek help from the psychologist Dr. Roger Vittoz in Lausanne had not abated. He was ready for a more radical step in his search for relief from these maladies of the soul. The spiritual pilgrimage of the abject subject dramatized in *The Waste Land* had not brought renewal. And it was clear that more intense psychological therapies were not the answer either. A decisive break was needed and there was no more radical a break than submission to God in an age increasingly devoted to the secular panaceas promised by the mechanized production of wellbeing through the wonders of chemistry, commodity consumption, and psychoanalysis. The Church would provide Eliot with the cultural and intellectual framework for the rest of his life. But it would not bring radical changes in the direction of his thinking about society, culture, and literature. Indeed, his migration to the Church seems in retrospect a wholly logical camber in the trajectory of his intellectual development.

Taken as a whole, Eliot's evolution derives from a limited number of early influences to which he was remarkably faithful throughout the rest of his life. His early devotion to the materialist discipline we now call anthropology, twinned with a curious loyalty to the philosophical idealism of F. H. Bradley, makes clear the paradox that runs through Eliot's life as well as his ideas. At the end it is the Christian doctrine of Incarnation, the involved union of matter and spirit, body and soul, as embodied by the Jesus Christ of the Gospels, that is the best single, historical instance of this fundamental paradox. A realization that certain kinds of Enlightenment rationality cannot grasp this paradox came to Eliot early in his intellectual development. His devotion to Bradley's metaphysics, though strong, was not finally defining. His use of a quotation from Bradley in the "Notes" to *The Waste Land* is often cited by scholars as evidence of the lasting influence of the British philosopher. But by 1922 Eliot was already past Bradley and the quotation acknowledges, perhaps even nostalgically, a past debt, a stage of development that is no longer actively running in the background of his present loci of attention. Later, his essay on Bradley in *For Lancelot Andrewes* (1928) looks back to the British philosopher as an influence, but by the late 1920s the influence is not philosophical as much as it is stylistic. It is Bradley's philosophical style, his pointedness, limpidity, and melancholy of thought and expression, which Eliot remembers. Within Eliot criticism there is a long and confused debate about Eliot's intellectual debt to Bradley. The tendency among critics is to cherrypick those ideas and formulations in Bradley that help in buttressing one or other interpretive gambit in dealing with Eliot's poems, especially the poetry up to *The Waste Land* and "The Hollow Men." But Eliot was not a systematic Bradleyan and by 1930 the influence of other thinkers is far more pronounced.

Philosophy

Eliot's New England connections brought a number of prominent philosophers to his attention through the general influence they exerted on American intellectual life. William Ellery Channing, Herbert Spencer, and Friedrich Schleiermacher were central, but it was Ralph Waldo Emerson who was the most famous among them and who exerted a kind of reverse influence on the young Eliot. Emerson's ideas were useful in the way that those with whom we disagree help us to understand better what we think and believe. Transcendentalism was not Eliot's cup of tea. Occasionally critics, such as Lee Oser, have tried to show that deep-down Eliot was an Emersonian in spite of himself.[3] But there is more wishful thinking in this judgment than fact. Later at Harvard, Eliot would find more congenial intellectual companionship with the New Realists, those who were opposed to Hegelianism and were profoundly influenced by the logical realism of Bertrand Russell. At Harvard Eliot came in productive contact with the personalities and works of George Santayana, Josiah Royce, Irving Babbitt, and William James. During his Paris year abroad in 1910–11, he also came in contact with Henri Bergson and for a time considered himself a Bergsonian until his taste for Bergson's ideas about the experience of time and of his semi-mystical belief in the workings of an *élan vital* faded and he became a decided anti-Bergsonian in his early London years. Charles Lanham and J. H. Woods at the university stimulated an interest in Indian philosophy and religion that continued throughout his life. The works of J. G. Frazer, Emile Durkheim, Max Müller, E. B. Tylor, Jane Harrison, and Lucien Lévy-Bruhl directed Eliot's attention from philosophy to the new disciplines of anthropology and sociology. The division between the two, and between both of them with philosophy, was not as clear then as it is today. Among the ancient philosophers, Eliot's advanced work was on Aristotle with Harold Joachim at Oxford. Later, the pre-Socratic Heraclitus would be given pride of place as the epigraphist of "Burnt Norton" and *Four Quartets*. Eliot's training in modern philosophy was not as extensive but he was aware of the early work in phenomenology in the writings of Edmund Husserl and Alexis Meinong.

Many critics and scholars refer to Eliot's philosophical training when reading his poetry. No doubt there are ways in which his interests in ideas have influenced his verse. But the wide variety of interpretations of how those ideas are actually manifested in his poetry suggests that perhaps poetry was not the preferred medium for the elaboration of his thinking. One could make the case that philosophy is far more important to his prose, both the critical works and his cultural criticism. Poetry, for Eliot, was the medium in which he worked out the practical consequences of action and belief. It was the discursive space where the messiness of life came up hard against ideals and concepts. The emphasis was on the mess and less on the formal elegance of ideas. It was in his prose that his conceptual imagination was most evident.

Culture and society

Although formally trained in philosophy, Eliot's more natural intellectual bent was toward what we would now call cultural criticism. The most complete statement of his views about culture and society was *Notes Towards the Definition of Culture*, published in 1948, but having been many decades in the making. Eliot's ideas may have begun to take formal shape during his Harvard years, but the fundamentals of his beliefs about the person, society, and the nature and reach of community, and his ideas about literature emerged, it is clear, from his life experience as much as from books and lectures in Cambridge, Massachusetts. Eliot was born into an aristocracy in democratic America, at least the only social elite that functioned as a kind of upper crust in that republican setting. His was one of the families, along with others like the Adams's or the Lowell's, that comprised a New England upper class. Society was not classless, even if it had egalitarianism as an ideal, and Eliot was very aware of the distinctions that make up a complex society. In 1948 he argued for the necessary existence of a functional social elite, an aristocracy of land and blood that was bred to provide the right kind of guidance for society. He did not argue for a form of authoritarianism, but for a traditionally hierarchical community in which distinctions of rank were not occasions for stimulating envy and rebellion but for recognizing their function in making and maintaining social stability. His social vision really looked back to the seventeenth and eighteenth centuries, where small rural communities achieved stability through the presence of social classes each helping to maintain the social whole. An aristocracy required the presence of those who could work the land, perhaps a peasantry, or yeoman farmers able to produce wealth and sustenance from the soil. The presence of a loyal and educated intellectual elite, such as clergymen, teachers, and poets, was also necessary. These were able to sustain a symbolic canopy of values and beliefs that immunized everyone, noble and commoner, from the modern malady of anomie. This small community needed a single faith, racial homogeneity, and a common language. From these elements a common culture could emerge that would help to position social and cultural identities. This was not simply a matter of ideas or values alone; there was for Eliot a geographical aspect as well. He believed that it was best that "the great majority of human beings should go on living in the place in which they were born" (*Notes* 52). Earlier, he had remarked in his editorializing in the *Criterion* and *After Strange Gods* that industrialism was a curse and that a return to the land would be the best antidote to what he considered pollution of the purity of ancient communities, the invasion of foreign races, urbanization and the social mobility that comes with it, and liberalism, the set of ideas that have unmoored personal identities from their foundations.

Notes Towards the Definition of Culture only puts more forcefully what was already evident in Eliot's other prose writings and in his poetry. In his poetry, for example, the mixing of races is never seen in any positive light. It is always a sign of social and cultural disintegration. In *Sweeney Agonistes*, "Gerontion," *The Waste Land*, "Burbank with a Baedeker," and other works, racial or ethnic heterogeneity marks the end of sociocultural harmony. The unraveling of kinship structures, the fragmentation of belief systems and the resulting loss of coherence, and the coming of what he called in an essay on "Rudyard Kipling" the unintelligibility of the industrialized mind leads inevitably to the end of society as he would like to have known it. The late nineteenth-century America in which Eliot was raised was the antithesis of the social ideal that he carried around in his head. Moreover, the England to which he migrated in 1914 was itself becoming the diversely multicultural society it is today. As a result, Eliot looked back in time and found what he believed to be the best embodiment of his ideas in Elizabethan England. The first few pages of his book of essays, *For Lancelot Andrewes* (1928), celebrate that historical moment as the high point of English civilization.

An individual is shaped by the culture into which he or she is born. Against the prejudice of modernity that defines the individual's life project as the struggle to realize one's uniqueness or, as the popular phrase has it, to find oneself, Eliot insisted on the exact opposite. Immersion in and conformity to a vital, historically grounded, traditional culture, one that encompasses not only the formal arts, but also the popular and life arts, such as music, house design, and cooking, is primarily what "makes life worth living" (*Notes* 27). Tradition gives a culture its sense of continuity and wholeness. "What I mean by tradition," Eliot wrote in *After Strange Gods*, "involves all those habitual actions, habits, and customs . . . which represent the blood kinship of 'the same people living in the same place'" (*ASG* 18), over, one might add, a long period of time. Blood and territorial kinship encompass both conscious elements of living, such as the love of *bocce* by rural Italians, and those that lie below consciousness and are woven into a community's fabric of existence, such as the grimacing twitch of the head among Greeks to convey assent. The emphasis on communal solidarity and cohesion offers individuals great strength by grounding identity in a concretely experienced common intuitive life.

It also has its toxic side, however, as evidenced by the *volkisch* nightmare of Germany in the 1930s and 1940s. The Nazi invocation of an exclusive folk culture favored an Aryan nation that was defined as the antithesis of the

"Others," the alien racial and social "pollutants," such as Jews, the Roma people, homosexuals, Slavs, and the disabled. In his thinking Eliot did not mean going the way of the Germans. Although he was influenced by European thinkers, like Charles Maurras, whose conservatism tended toward fascism, Eliot was as horrified by the Nazi perversion of conservative ideology as anyone else in liberal Europe. Nevertheless, there lurks in this invocation of blood, soil, and tradition the danger of tying the bonds of nation and community so tightly that they both strangle the chosen populace and dehumanize the outsiders.

In this area Eliot's ideas reacted against the nineteenth-century habit, found in its most eloquent form in the cultural criticism of Matthew Arnold, of thinking of culture as the framework of human life. Eliot could not agree. For him, religion was the key, not simply as a form of cultural expression but rather as a supernatural power finding expression, not as culture, but as something spiritually immanent in the worldly state. Religion grounds the values that Eliot endorsed, not religion as transcendence, but religion as woven into concrete existence *via* institutions, historical practices, sacred texts, and those specially trained in the maintenance of the faith. Human society was both material and spiritual at the same time, very much like the concept of Incarnation in Christian belief. Christ is the model. And society is no different; it is the worldly presence of a supernatural reality. Thus those ideologies that are purely materialistic or basically social, such as communism and liberalism, distort reality. Similarly, human beings are both concrete individuals and spirits. The modern habit of emphasizing the merely existential character of the individual immersed in social, economic, and political contexts limits and disfigures humanity. It emphasizes all those aspects of the personality that are shaped by worldly contingency. For the genuine self to emerge, one must get past personality, an abstraction manifested by the superficialities of fashionable clothes, streaked hair, and sexy cars.

Romanticism and classicism

It was from these ideas about society that Eliot's thinking about the arts and about poetry in particular took its primary colorings. He challenged the dominant Romantic conception of art in the nineteenth century at the very point where sociality intersects with personal identity. He saw that for the Romantic artist, personality is the key term, the individual context from which art emerges. Eliot took a very different view in his important essay of 1919, "Tradition and the Individual Talent." Attendance to the medium and to the necessary craft lays the proper foundation for the making of art. In this Eliot put into practice the ideas he found in de Gourmont and T. E. Hulme. They sketched the outline of a thoroughgoing classicism as counterpoint to the dominant ego-based Romanticism of the age.

As a result, the practice of poetry is not simply self-expression, but something more objective, something "impersonal," to use Eliot's word. Indeed, the creative or poetic process cannot be focused on the projection of a personality, no matter how interesting the personal experience of the poet: one must work to escape from personality. The poet must attend to the medium first and foremost. In the poet's mind language is transformed into something other than self-expression. The imagination functions like a catalyst in a chemical reaction. It is necessary for the reaction to take place but it is not itself the product of the reaction. This conception of the imagination challenged the nineteenth-century view, primarily expressed by Samuel Taylor Coleridge, which saw the imagination as the highest function of the mind. Eliot regarded such theories as immature and believed that the poet must concentrate on a "practical sense of realities" (*SE* 275) rather than being rapt by his or her own experiences.

Such a conception of tradition and the individual corresponds with a conservative social vision that stresses continuity with and loyalty to the past over and above the prize of uniqueness, of individuality. Challenging this and other modern commonplaces, Eliot believed that the history of the West was one of decline from the high point of medieval culture, which allowed Dante to produce great art from a fully integrated, classical civilization, to a culture that had lost its bearings in the tangles of liberalism, cultivation of the ego, and pervasive cynicism. This historical narrative of decline, or what he called "cultural breakdown" in *Notes Towards the Definition of Culture* (105), may stimulate cultural pessimism, but that was not the end of the story of the contemporary world. The new writing of the first decades of the twentieth century – the writings of Joyce, Lewis, H. D., Pound, and, of course, Eliot himself – represent a countercultural modernism that has the power to transform literature and to open a path toward a reinvigoration of the classical inheritance that Eliot saw so well represented in Dante. This view made the promotion of the new writing through the encouragement of publishing enterprises and through efforts to place the work of comrades in journals not only a commitment to helping one's friends but an aspect of the cultural politics of the early twentieth century. The "culture wars" or the conflict of values that is still part of the political discourse of the early twenty-first century have one of their starting points in Eliot's time.

In the narrative of cultural decline, Eliot felt that he had found the historical moment when the breakdown could be seen most clearly. The Renaissance cult of exuberant rhetoric and the even more exuberant display of the individual ego as irrepressible personality broke step with the past, especially the classical clarity and cohesion of the Middle Ages. In that early historical moment, one could argue, as Eliot did, that the person was shaped by a civilization in which intellect, emotion, and spirituality were unified. During the Renaissance, a separation begins to set in and intellect, emotion, spiritual experience, one's place in the social order, and other aspects of self-identity, drift apart in a process that Eliot called the "dissociation of sensibility" ("The Metaphysical Poets," [1921], *SE* 288). For Eliot, this occurs in the seventeenth century. John Donne in the earlier part of that century is one of the last poets to exemplify the virtues of a unified sensibility. For Donne, thought was not simply a disembodied abstraction, it was an experience. He "possessed a mechanism of sensibility which could devour any kind of experience" (*SE* 287–288). Yet at the very moment that Donne was experiencing thought with the same sensuousness and vitality as one might savor the scent of a rose, the forces that would lead to dissociation were already at work in embryonic form. John Milton stands as the first great poet of a ruined inner world and Eliot did everything he could to shake the reputation of a figure venerated in English literature for two centuries. In Eliot's view, Milton's work was the product of a mind seduced by its own desire for self-display, and this is not simply a fault of character in Milton; it is part of a wider cultural decline that Milton reflects more fully than most. The rhetoric of his greatest poetry was unhealthy and ruined the style of later writers when they tried to imitate him. Although his language has become more refined, Eliot argued, it has lost the fluency and clarity of a Dante and become cloyed, clouded, and eccentric because feeling has become cruder. In addition, his characters are not fully mature and his Satan in *Paradise Lost* does not stand up to comparison with Christopher Marlowe's Mephistofeles. It was in these terms that Eliot argued for a reevaluation of the literary tradition of England with the aim of displacing a writer like Milton from the eminence he had achieved in the eighteenth and nineteenth centuries. In this task he was followed by a number of eminent scholars such as F. R. Leavis.

Milton may have been easy to abuse, but William Shakespeare did not escape implication in the story of cultural breakdown. Eliot acknowledged Shakespeare's genius on a number of occasions but found that without the intellectual and affective supports of an integrated culture, much like Dante enjoyed in *trecento* Italy, Shakespeare's genius never acquired the kind of classical discipline that made Dante's *The Divine Comedy* the greatest literary work in the European tradition. To prove his point Eliot tackled Shakespeare's greatest play, *Hamlet,* in the essay "Hamlet and his Problems" (1921). In this landmark text Eliot argued that the play was disfigured by Shakespeare's inability to balance the total sum of feeling projected by Hamlet with the created character. Some "intractable material" in Hamlet's character could not be dramatized. The emotional content overcame the dramatic form, leaving us with a sense of imbalance, lack of control, and a sense of unreality. From this analysis Eliot drew one of his most important critical ideas, the concept of "objective correlative." The general point has become a classic formulation:

> The only way of expressing emotion in the form of art is by finding an "objective correlative"; in other words, a set of objects, a situation, a chain of events which shall be the formula of that *particular* emotion; such that when the external facts, which must terminate in sensory experience, are given, the emotion is immediately evoked.
>
> (*SW* 100, italics in original)

We can see Eliot's predisposition to classical standards in this definition. Inspiration is not unregulated emotional exuberance. It is highly controlled, balanced, and objective. He never repudiated this formulation, though in 1947 he confessed to being surprised, that the idea had found wide acceptance in criticism.

Shakespeare's problem with *Hamlet* was not put down to a lack of talent or inspiration on Shakespeare's part. The problem may have had a technical manifestation in the drawing of a character in a play, but it was Shakespeare's society that let him down. Shakespeare was a genius, the equal of any artist living or dead, but some of the other giants of European literature (Dante, for instance) had the benefit of a great culture to sustain them. Shakespeare, Milton, and the Romantics did not. The new social and political forces of the Renaissance undermined the kind of control on which an artist fully integrated with a poised civilization could rely. So that Shakespeare is not to blame for any flaws in his work; the cultural support system in which he worked let him down. This underlines the importance that Eliot always placed on the particular contexts in which poets and artists worked, which meant that technical matters in composition were not limited to the craft or inspiration of a particular poet. Even minor poets could produce work of quality if the social and cultural environment was right. The creative act is not limited to a few isolated geniuses living on metaphorical mountain peaks of inspiration producing works of art whole from their overheated imaginations. Acts of due deliberation, attention to the medium, and control of one's materials are as important, according to Eliot, as the volcanic power of imagination celebrated by the Romantics and their successors.

A sense of the past

These ideas ran against the grain of another commonplace of modernity, the notion that history is progressive, that time inevitably sees the improvement of life, culture, and morals. Yet for Eliot, the advances in technology and in the increasing ease and comfort of living should not be mistaken for the moral or intellectual improvement of human beings. In fact, Eliot believed that modernity had ruptured its connection to a more vital past and was as a result impoverished. History is not continuous progress but is characterized, instead, by ruptures and retrogression. On this issue Eliot was not only out of step with contemporary thought, especially the dominant liberalism, but, paradoxically, he was also ahead of his time. In the twenty-first century we have finally caught up with Eliot's sense of history as rupture rather than continuity and with his sense that after periods of seeming progress, history goes into reverse and moves in retrogressive ways. Take industrialism, for example. It has opened panoramas of technical mastery that were inconceivable when Eliot was born, yet the fallout of unbridled industrial expansion has taken us backward as well as forward. The environmental waste lands that appear in urban areas as a result of rapid industrial expansion are a case in point. Sadder still is the fact that the ecological mistakes of the past do not always lead to wiser action in the future. To visit the new industrial cities of China today is in a sense to time-travel back to the Manchester of the 1850s in England.

Such notions complicated Eliot's sense of the past, especially in the particulars of tradition. This returns us to that most important of his essays, "Tradition and the Individual Talent." There his idea of tradition is strangely unprogressive. The liberal sense of the cultural past is keyed to the idea of improvement and it is this very concept that he labors to attack in the opening paragraphs of the essay. The poet

> must be aware that the mind of Europe – the mind of his own country – a mind which he learns in time to be much more important than his own private mind – is a mind which changes, and that this change is a development which abandons nothing *en route*, which does not superannuate either Shakespeare, or Homer, or the rock drawing of the Magdalenian draughtsmen. That this development, refinement perhaps, complication certainly, is not, from the point of view of the artist, any improvement. (*SE* 6)

The contemporary artist is not at the head of the class simply because he comes chronologically after the artists of the past. Homer is as much his contemporary in the present as Elton John. The "dead writers," he goes on to say, are distanced from us because we "*know* so much more than they." But "they are that which we know" (*SE* 6). The idea that a new work of art "has a simultaneous existence and composes a simultaneous order" (*SE* 4) departs radically from the Romantic commonplace that it is the duty of the inspired artist to give birth to the absolutely unique and original work, a work whose singularity is defined by its distance from and nonconformity with all other works of art.

The idea of simultaneity in Eliot's sense leads him to the most radical formulation in this essay. Every artist finds himself or herself in some relation to those who have gone before. The value of the artist's work is arrived at by the method of compare and contrast as an aesthetic principle, not simply as a matter of historical or period differences. The literary critical concept of "influence," it seems, flows in two ways, from the past to the present and vice versa, from the present back to the past. Once you have read the first line of *The Waste Land*, you cannot read the opening lines of Chaucer's "General Prologue" in *The Canterbury Tales* in the same way again. Tradition is not a chronology, a succession or a series, it is always complete and the new work alters, even in small ways, all the other works in the set of existing "monuments." In this way, the value of any one work is found in the fact of its inclusion in the set, that is, its proximity to all other works, not by its distance from them.

These germinal ideas which Eliot gathered from his nineteenth-century predecessors and various contemporaries stimulated a number of new critical theories and practices in the twentieth century. Practical criticism in England and the "new criticism" in America are not entirely the products of Eliot's thought, but they would be rather different without his critical interventions in the early years of the century. Behind them stand traditions of reading and writing that date back to the Middle Ages. These defined the parallel critical "classicism" that the poetry of Eliot and his modernist contemporaries – Joyce, Lewis, Pound, and others – saw as their special task in reviving what for them were moribund traditions not only of literature, but more generally of a whole culture.

Chapter 3

Works

T. S. Eliot was a poet first and a critic second. We remember Eliot the poet more often in our time because of the steady interest in his poetry. With the evolution of critical thinking, his criticism is studied for its historical importance rather than for its own sake. But we cannot conceive of the contemporary critical milieu without acknowledging his important early role in creating it. His critical writings were not limited to the study of literature or literary culture – he was also a social critic and commentator on politics and religion. Although we normally divide his work into two broad categories, poetry and prose, we ought to resist the temptation to make this division hard and fast. In fact, Eliot's poetry and prose are of a piece; one is really inconceivable without the other. An account of the leading themes in his work must therefore join the poetry and criticism together, while at the same time being sensitive to the differences that make them distinct.

Their differences originate in Eliot's two earliest intellectual passions, his personal interest in poetry and his academic interest in philosophy. Poetry and philosophy are quite obviously distinct modalities of thought and feeling, yet the two are not entirely disconnected. Both tackle the fundamental questions of existence, namely the nature and course of experience and knowledge. Both foreground the activities of consciousness and both raise the question of the poet's or thinker's own subjectivity as an imaginative construct and as a warping effect on thought. The most apt metaphor is probably the coin, two sides of the same thing, and that is precisely the relation that poetry and philosophy bear to Eliot's intellectual evolution. He was drawn to philosophy for the same reason that many find it appealing. In a generally untidy world, the cool and methodical reasoning of the professional thinker has its attractions, principal among them the pull of reason itself. The orderly movements of the philosophical mind will no doubt fascinate those who are acutely aware of the world's unsettling dishevelment. The strength of ideas and the systems they inspire, and philosophy's calming assurances in setting down certainties for the inquiring spirit (even the certainty of uncertainty), are all blessings of the highest kind in the traditions of Western thought. The Socratic rejection of the prevailing semi-mystical character of early Greek thought and Socrates's skepticism toward the Greek religion gave birth to Western philosophy through the achievement of Plato and Aristotle. From that starting point Western philosophy found itself grounded in reason and logic. The epiphanic, visionary, and imaginative activities of the mind were ruled out of order by the new philosophy as a path toward the truth.

By all subsequent accounts, that moment in Athens four hundred years before the Common Era was a great leap forward. Indeed, it has been generally celebrated as a triumph. But it came with a cost. The philosophers Friedrich Nietzsche and Martin Heidegger have famously dissented from this view of the development of Western thought. The problem is that the domain of philosophical inquiry narrowed significantly as a result of the Socratic revolution in thinking. When the Greek mind took that step, it suddenly, and some might say catastrophically, separated theology, poetry, and philosophy into distinct compartments. We cannot disentangle theology, poetry, and philosophy in the works of the pre-Socratics, thinkers such as Parmenides, Heraclitus, and Anaximander. Theology, poetry, and philosophy were a single discipline before Socrates. At this remove in time, we cannot recreate the intellectual climate in which this integration of knowledge was not only possible, but experienced as inevitable. We know that after Socrates, and thanks to the authority of Plato, who banned the poet from his ideal Republic, there was no place for poetry in the new rational order of things. Whether this separation and categorizing is a blessing or curse is difficult to say.

As a student, Eliot simply accommodated himself to the situation of thought which he inherited, though later he came to see the separation of thought and feeling, what he called the "dissociation of sensibility," as disastrous for the mind of Europe. But when young, his philosophical studies led him in the direction of the rationalist systematizing of Western metaphysics known as Idealism. Pursuit of the Ideal and of the twin concept of the Absolute brought Eliot to the limits of the knowable which, in turn, led inevitably to the need to violate the boundary that separates philosophy from the spiritual world, the boundary that separates ratiocination from modes of apprehension beyond language and logic. Eliot did not turn to mystical theology as such, but he was led to explore in his poetry the domain beyond that which the mind or the senses could rationally grasp. That domain, he soon came to learn, is also beyond the reach of language.

Schooled in the philosophical culture of his time, Eliot tackled the principal topics of his formal studies: the opposition between realism and idealism, the dialectic of the One and the Many, the nature of the Self and its relationship to the external world, the unity (or not) of thought and feeling, and the need to find the common ground among spirituality, poetry, and philosophy. To these he added his own leaven, the question of language. In this latter interest he was in advance of his time. The twentieth century launched the linguistic turn in the human sciences and Eliot found himself in the vanguard of that historic philosophical moment.

Yet this direction was not simply the product of philosophical study. His birth on the Mississippi River at a social and political crossroads brought him to a concrete awareness of language and culture from birth. Eliot's birth into a prominent family with roots in Boston and the New England of the early pilgrims was an important element in his socialization in language as a young man. Protestant piety and an unadorned prose defined one of the discursive standards of the Massachusetts colony in the seventeenth century. The other was a religious rhetoric of considerable visionary intensity that derived from the heated doctrinal politics of Reformation and Counter-Reformation Europe that had been played out violently in England in the Civil War of the 1640s and the Commonwealth under Cromwell that followed it. Piety, preaching, and public service became, for the Eliots, a family tradition. In this respect they were much like other Massachusetts pilgrim families. The proliferating branches of the family tree were meticulously recorded by the Eliots and in 1887, when the genealogical map was printed, its extent, with its many prominent family members and the connections to other notable American families, established beyond any doubt the Eliots' claim to being one of the more distinguished families in America.

Yet the aristocratic bearing clashed with the revolutionary, republican, and democratic instincts and traditions of the American nation. Although high pretensions could be carried off more comfortably in stuffy New England, they were a little more difficult to sustain in dusty, blunt-speaking Missouri. There the claims of pedigree lost something of their New England charm and may have seemed somewhat ridiculous under the hot Missouri sun. For his family, the sense of noble purpose, duty, responsibility, and high-mindedness persisted, but it ran up hard against the reality of a tough, newly industrialized city that still had, in pockets, the feel of a frontier town about it. This comingling of city and frontier, gentles and "savages,"[1] the proximity of modern civilization with the ancient culture of aboriginal tribes, the bare-knuckle democracy of the wilderness, and the freebooting push of rootless men, were to press on Eliot a fundamental partitioning of experience that manifested itself in myriad ways through the rest of his life and in his writing. An early upbringing in these circumstances not only affected his poetry but influenced in particular his social and cultural criticism as well. It does not explain the sources of his ideas about the uses of poetry and prose, but life on the Mississippi, at a crucial moment in the evolution of American culture, provided Eliot with an ethos from within which the strength of his subsequent ideas and the polemical emphases of the later intellectual commitments can be more easily assessed.

Eliot's immersion in the American language took a new twist when he found himself at Harvard. In St. Louis the Eliots were an elite family; in Boston Tom was surrounded by the scions of the New England Brahminate. He was no longer on top of the social heap by virtue of his family's pedigree. In New England all the boys into whose company he was thrust had equally distinguished bloodlines and connections. In Missouri his family's social position and his delicate health made him something of an outsider, but it was a comfortable remoteness fashioned by privilege. In Boston he faced a different dilemma. His speech, infused with a Missouri twang, marked him as an outsider in a new way. There was nothing comfortable about the taint of provincialism that accompanied the flat vowels of his accent. Some adolescents, with a more rebellious streak in them, might have pressed home their difference from their fellows. Eliot, in the social maneuver that would later acclimatize him to Britain, simply changed the way he spoke. Later in life, the words "provincial" or "provincialism," tainted by the experience of disquiet in adolescence, would invariably take on a pejorative association for Eliot.

A curiosity and wariness about language and culture emerges very early in Eliot's intellectual life. It comes in comments and observations in papers that he wrote during his university years and in his doctoral thesis, *Knowledge and Experience in the Philosophy of F. H. Bradley* (1916). But this focus on language took its most important form, not in his philosophical studies *per se*, but in his poetry and in his criticism. The causes of this turn to language in the twentieth century are many and complex but perhaps the single most important reason for a poet, the one that captures the mood of Eliot's early and even some of his late poetry, has been described best by the German philosopher Heidegger in his comments about the spoliation of language as a vital medium for connection in modern times. He argues that in modernity, "language in general is worn out and used up – an indispensable but masterless means of communication that may be used as one pleases, as indifferent as a means of public transport, as a street car which everyone rides in. Everyone speaks and writes away in the language, without hindrance and above all *without danger*."[2]

Heidegger goes on to say that only "a very few" are able to bring language back to life from the death-in-life into which it has fallen in modern times. This is the special task of poets and Eliot seems to have understood this as his own particular poetic task. The possibilities of making poetry from a fallen language, a language exhausted by use, worn down by the nonstop traffic in pedestrian chatter and triteness, was suggested by his reading of the poetry of Charles Baudelaire and Jules Laforgue.

Early poems

This conception of his task can be seen in an early poem like "Conversation Galante" (*CP* 35) published in his first collection in 1917, *The Love Song of J. Alfred Prufrock and Other Observations*. Framed as a stilted dialogue about the moon, music, and miscommunication between two lovers, the poem heightens our sense of the inveterate languageness of experience. Contact between the two lovers is mediated by the labored metaphors about the moon. They foreground the impossibility of getting past a language used up by the standard clichés we associate with such a scene. The poem makes us conscious of the world as a cardboard stage with pretty characters posed in self-conscious imitation of the sentimental lovers one might find in an Elizabethan play. These are not the witty lovers of Shakespeare, the Beatrice and Benedict of *Much Ado About Nothing*, for example. These represent a dreary Hero and a vacuous Claudio. The care that is taken in how the language is put into circulation and the relation between experience and the words that both construct and interpret it are clear loci of attention in the poem. The emphasis on what is said by the two lovers in the first few lines attunes us quickly to the languageness of experience, while implying at a deeper level a philosophical problem of wide compass. The poem satirizes a situation of reticence, misunderstanding, and coyness, which would become a stock scene in Eliot's early poetry. It unveils a society where life seems little more than a masquerade, an empty ritual of idle talk and narcissism.

In order to understand in greater detail the satiric uses to which Eliot put much of his earlier poetry, we need to understand the upper-middle-class social milieu, especially the manners and mores of New England, which provided Eliot with his experiences as an adolescent and as a young man. He learned early, as did "Miss Helen Slingsby" (*CP* 31) the "secret codes" of this world. But his attitude toward this environment was ambivalent. He both enjoyed the benefits that such a world had to offer him – a Harvard education, study abroad, and so on – and loathed them. Enough at least to grasp any excuse not to return when he escaped to continental Europe and England in 1914. Although he found himself in avant-garde circles in London in his first English years, his changing religious sensibilities moved him toward more socially central affiliations. There was a rough equivalence between Eliot's social destination in England and his social origins in America. His experience of emigration from America to England was keyed by his sense of America as "a family extension" of England, so that his migration was from the peripheries of a culture back to its center.[3]

From this view of its origins, Eliot's America had come into being as the consequence of a number of sociopolitical transformations in England in the seventeenth century. In virtual isolation, as early as the 1620s the pilgrims and earliest settlers had begun to erect a sort of paternalistic culture from the least promising fragments of English social and religious life in the seventeenth century. Later, the Puritan *émigrés* were people who could not stomach or survive the political and social settlements in Restoration England at the end of the century. These fragments, whose affective experience was determined by their genesis in opposition to the established continuities of English royalism and the Church of England, also turned out to be the most open to Enlightenment ideas in the eighteenth century, through which the hinterland finally glimpsed an acceptable, republican future for itself. As an Enlightenment extension of Europe, having never lost its sense of inferiority to the source culture, the American bourgeoisie in Eliot's youth stiffened into social roles and behavior cut to a pattern drawn in England. Such behavior was inherently contradictory. England was both desired as a pattern of culture and manners, and rejected. In this contradiction we can see the true character of the colonial mentality, a mixture of abject, and humiliating, mimicry wedded to impotent gestures of defiance. Eliot learned how to follow the emotional lurches of this paradox with uncanny precision.

Characteristic of this particular experience in the New England of his student days is the poem "Mr. Apollinax" (*CP* 33). It illustrates his punishingly severe attitude toward his own social antecedents. The poem places England and New England side by side. "Mr. Apollinax" is conventionally read as Eliot's response to the visit of the British philosopher Bertrand Russell to Harvard in early 1914. The relation between the "irresponsible foetus" (Apollinax) and Boston gentility, among whom Apollinax's "centaur hoofs" beat "over the hard turf," is sharply delineated. Russell is "laughter," a transsexual blend of "Fragilion" and "Priapus," "submarine and profound," "the old man of the sea . . . Hidden under coral islands," a head "grinning over a screen / With seaweed in its hair." The sexual composite that brings together Fragilion (a name suggesting an effeminate man), the robust virility of Priapus, and the reference to the centaur makes of Apollinax a dangerous and alluring intruder in a well-bred world. But he is not only a force of disquieting, sexualized energy. He is also a mischievous, mercurial intellectual, to be experienced in all the sudden and delightful aspects that his wit showers on his startled hosts. He embodies an energy that only metaphor can hope to enclose, as he beats around the shrubbery and the teacups, provoking in the anxious "Mrs. Phlaccus" and the uncomprehending "Professor and Mrs. Cheetah" polite retreats.

The conception of irrepressible, authentic being in terms of myth is also noteworthy as it anticipates the attempted integration of symbolic totalities in *The Waste Land* (1922). But, for the time being, myth here functions socially, not epistemologically. It provides an absolute reference, both rational and rapturous, Apollonian and Dionysian, to be juxtaposed – with humor and more than a little satisfied disdain – with the appalled smiles of New England marionettes. If the abounding energy of Apollinax can be enclosed only by the play of metaphor, which associates him with an authentic profundity, intellectual and mythic, his alarmed hosts are contained metonymically, in the minor props of their world: such things as "a slice of lemon," "a bitten macaroon," and the brittle talk: "'He is a charming man' . . . 'There was something he said that I might have challenged.'" While his "dry and passionate" presence devours the afternoon, the sere, oppressive social milieu answers only with incomprehension and impotence. The dead husks of conversation at the end of the poem do not simply register fear and dislike of Apollinax, but express the social affirmations and solidarity of a social class, putting aright their little world violated and bruised by the visitor.

All the poems in *Prufrock and Other Observations* expose and subvert psychologically the solidities and certainties of that upper middle-class-world in which Eliot was raised. Perhaps the word "observations" in the title

underlines the intent. Many of the poems resemble those peculiarly vulner-
able moments when, on opening a door, someone catches sight of a gesture
or a look that suddenly makes vividly clear a hidden secret or hypocrisy or
self-delusion.

> The Dresden clock continued ticking on the mantelpiece,
> And the footman sat upon the dining-table
> Holding the second housemaid on his knees –
> Who had always been so careful while her mistress lived.
>
> ("Aunt Helen," *CP* 31)

These poems are dense with the knowledge of the textures, decors, voices,
glances, speech habits, in short the entire physical, verbal, moral, emotional
sediment – the "dust in crevices" ("Rhapsody on a Windy Night," *CP* 28) – of
a whole way of life. Here again, details can be divided into two sorts of
figurative event according to function. Some are clearly metaphorical,
directed toward symbolizing in outward terms inward uncertainties and
hesitations. The curious silence in heaven and on earth after Aunt Helen's
death is a good example of that. Indeed, the uncertainty (as deliberate theme,
not as psychological fact) goes so far in many cases (and we shall see this in
greater depth in "The Love Song of J. Alfred Prufrock") that it engulfs the
metaphorical process itself in a kind of backwash of anxiety. Until *Ash-
Wednesday* the Eliotic metaphor, when it is deployed at all, is always made
to totter on the edge of self-extinction. That Eliot was able to make great
poetry from this tropic wobble is itself a remarkable achievement.

Images and narrative events in these early poems also function metonymically. They defer metaphor by shifting the interpretive focus to the
social ethos from which the poem draws its props. A "Dresden clock" is
both a Dresden clock and a decorous metonymy for a whole way of life, a
life that Eliot clearly knew his readers would instantly place. He knew they
would hear, in the specificity of the reference, the banal music of a conventional existence that includes the predictable middle-class suspicion of what
the servants are always up to behind the scenes. All the details in the poem
function metonymically to situate the lived density of this way of life, and
not only the objects, but also the small social acts, such as the open ease of
the footman and housemaid in the absence of their mistress. Certainly, the
irony of the servants' behavior is directed at subverting Aunt Helen's
propriety, but the irony, as a metonymic sign, also exposes the blindness
of a whole social class. Eliot's metaphors may choke quietly and ambigu-
ously in the dust, but there is no doubt about the music of his barbed
metonymies.

As readers of poetry, we tend to notice the metaphors; rarely do we attend to the possibilities of a metonymic approach. In his management of the affective content of "pure" images, Eliot was able to sketch from the concrete experiences and objects of everyday life a portrait of an age. In this respect he discovered a methodology in the writing of poems that parallels coincidentally the method of film or cinema discourse. Eliot's use of the image as typifying metonymy is a practice of immense importance because it allows the text to offer concrete objects and experiences as particular images and, at the same, evoke the bigger picture of time and place of which they are a part. In literary criticism the image is interpreted as the minimal unit of *aesthetic* perception in modernism. Eliot awakened and exploited the potential of the image to function metonymically in a social context. In his poetry, therefore, the image serves more than aesthetic function. As a typifying element, a revealing particular, the image becomes impossible to dissociate from the socioethical concepts and ideas, or forms of concrete life, which it typifies.

Of course, "Mr. Apollinax" and "Aunt Helen" and the other poems in Eliot's early collections do not simply raise a mirror to their milieu. The poems do not innocently reproduce the daft foibles of a dotty society. The social world, as seen by Eliot's poetic personae, is certainly full of low comedy, and no one seems exempt from it, including his speakers. In "Portrait of a Lady" the speaking voice wearily elaborates a kind of uneasy distance from a world of motiveless caprice. The speaker sits reading "the comics" and "the sporting page" of a newspaper. He lists in the haphazard manner of newspaper layout a number of unconnected stories and events. All is calm and "self-possessed" until the worn-out melody of a "street-piano" undermines his composure. ("Portrait of a Lady," *CP* 20–21). But the loss of self-possession marks an important shift in the piling up of disconcerting detail. The speaker is invaded by the very caprice that the newspaper iterates. The satirist, it seems, cannot evade the notice of his own satire, because he cannot avoid speaking the language of the world he satirizes. Neither can the more purely lyrical voice of the traditional love song any longer escape the conventional hysterics of melodrama.

> Clasp your flowers to you with a pained surprise –
> Fling them to the ground and turn
> With a fugitive resentment in your eyes:
>
> ("La Figlia Che Piange," *CP* 36)

Moments of genuine rapture are still possible: "Her hair over her arms and her arms full of flowers." But the intellectual clarity of the love poets of thirteenth-century Tuscany or eleventh-century Provence has vanished. Their clarity and rigor returns only in fits and starts, in individual lines and fragments. The rest is all defection and banality, or, at worst, the preposterous pretensions of a feckless egoism.

These early poems powerfully foreground the customs, beliefs, emotional reflexes, and conduct of Eliot's immediate New England milieu and they do this in order to make his readers see them anew. His methods aim at displacement as a technique that unsettles the sediment of an established life. They are also fragments of spiritual autobiography, a record of a struggle that cannot decide easily whether ridicule or dread is the best way of surviving middle-class anxieties. The poems certainly record the action of well-marked anxieties, but they do so in order to make more visible the conventional language games that sustain them. This is a new kind of poetry in English (though not in French); a poetry made by the avoidance of poetry. Or to put it more exactly, Eliot's poems deliberately evoke the excesses of a dying Romanticism in order to push them aside, to displace them. This will become a standard practice for him throughout his career. The Romantic legacy was still very much in evidence in Eliot's time. It presented soulful self-expression as the major note of its affective style. It was also entrepreneurially egotistical, comfortably subjective, fashionably neurotic, and, to be honest, dead witless.

"Portrait of a Lady"

In "Portrait of a Lady" poetry is made by the ironic foregrounding of all these hollow materials. The method is unrelenting. It pervades, for example, the rhythmic shaping of the lines and makes the possibility of an innocent and conventionally pretty verse music impossible.

> – And so the conversation slips
> Among velleities and carefully caught regrets
> Through attenuated tones of violins
> Mingled with remote cornets
> And begins.   ("Portrait of a Lady," *CP* 18)

The rhythmic effect of the fourth line ("Mingled with remote cornets") is self-consciously engulfed by the wider irony, with the result that a possibly beautiful line is transformed; we hear the *effect* itself as a sign of a debased verbal coinage. By raising its own often masterfully constructed effects as tokens of a debauched currency, the poem is able to focus more clearly and more devastatingly the etiolated and disembodied character of the personal relationship it enacts.

The epigraph from Christopher Marlowe's *The Jew of Malta* with its evocation of biblical ethics, "Thou has committed," and the brutal candor of the following word, accentuated by the pause – "Fornication . . ." (18) contrasts with the "velleities" of a submerged eroticism that cannot find any possible outward expression, except in oblique and deflected forms, in, as it were, symbolic couplings, like "friendship."

> 'You do not know how much they mean to me, my friends,
> And how, how rare and strange it is, to find
> In a life composed so much, so much of odds and ends,
> (For indeed I do not love it . . . you knew? you are not blind!
> How keen you are!)
> To find a friend who has these qualities,
> Who has, and gives
> Those qualities upon which friendship lives.   (18–19)

Here is the carefully coded speech of the salon, formulaically sincere, but alert to how words silently mobilize consent, silently convey an unspeakable duplicity at work of which the male persona is only obscurely aware. The tentative and precarious movement of the woman's conversation proceeds by repetitions, interruptions, qualifications, and an exacting syntax. These are the signs she offers of "a life composed so much," but not, as she says, of "odds and ends." This tactical evocation of a distracted spontaneity veils the actual severity of the composition, subtextually signaled in the exact affective shaping of the syntax – "To find a friend who has these qualities, / Who has, and gives / Those qualities . . ." – the phrase "and gives" here catching up the merest ghost of a possibly concrete demand, to be immediately dissolved in the generality that follows. Calculation has become the hidden origin of authenticity.

We return to the epigraph like a drowning man. Among the windings of these violins, all that seems solid one moment melts into air in the next. What the poem does is unmask the subtle and delicate shell game that underlies the genuine. In the distance between the biblical-Elizabethan candor of "Fornication" and the fabricated candor of the love affair lies all the poem's force. The blunt tone of the epigraph functions as the measure against which the false notes are compared. The greater efficacy of the epigraph's tone marks a more genuine candor, a more compelling social speech, and a more musical poetic speech than the desiccated husks of ritualized intimacies.

The inertial drag of the ritual, a weight that progressively paralyzes the male speaker, provides a baseline for the play of an ambiguous eroticism which the woman commands. These social rituals and boundaries become the occasion for the gratuitous provocation of desire. The erotic glimmers to life when the woman's talk, or the man's, seems to threaten transgression of the boundaries, in what amounts to, for this context at least, a risky testing of the thin membrane that separates the push of a possibly anarchic desire and the coyly deferred promise of its breach in some actual human contact.

Eliot's epigraph cuts through these tangles like a clean wire. Its voice shows us how we are to take the represented events. In its biblical and Elizabethan evocations, it also serves to locate historically the poem's enactments. It reminds us of that premodern world in which codes of conduct and affect were not assumed to be arbitrary or contingent. With their origins obscured, these codes now stimulate desire artificially, and, worse still, the poem suggests, not even for the sake of its final satisfaction, but for the purpose of observing its disembodied motions at a distance. This drawing-room pornography is decisively reproved by an earlier form of moral and sexual directness to which the epigraph points. The precise character of this sexuality, the "platonic libertinism" of late nineteenth-century middle-class culture, has been well described by Peter Gay. In writing of bourgeois sexual experience and knowledge in that time, he asserts that "there was a great deal of innuendo, often in surprising places, conveying not sexual information so much as an atmosphere of sensuality, of a vague ferment . . . The well-brought up and the comfortable knew rather more than they were willing to reveal to others, or acknowledge to themselves."[4]

"The Love Song of J. Alfred Prufrock"

"The Love Song of J. Alfred Prufrock" operates in the same psychoethical regions as "Portrait of a Lady," but with greater penetration and reach.[5] In one respect the poem has already seen past the psychological construction of the self: although psychology was a new discipline at that time, Eliot even then anticipated a postmodern construction of personal identity. Years later, he was to describe this new condition of personhood more explicitly in his essay on the poet Lord Byron. Eliot perceived in Byron his making of "a self that is largely a deliberate fabrication – a fabrication that is only completed in the actual writing of the lines" (*PP* 203). Prufrock, like Byron, devotes "immense trouble to *becoming* a role" (205, italics in original), but, unlike Byron, Prufrock, performing what is now a clownish routine, can no longer carry off "such a useless and petty purpose" with the heroic persistence of a Byron (203). In the hundred years that separate Prufrock from Childe Harold,

Byron's heroic masquerade suffuses the whole of society but with its heroism in tatters. Prufrock does not exist except as a personality saturated in the vapid egoism that pervades masculinity at every level, from its sociopolitical heights, in a character like the "romantic aristocrat" George Wyndham (comically deflated by Eliot in *The Sacred Wood*, 24–32), down to the faceless, sad clerks in offices. This conscious exploration of the self as a "deliberate fabrication" does not actually begin with Eliot. The Victorian poet Arthur Hugh Clough skirted the same terrain in the character of his antihero Claude, in *Amours de Voyage* (1920).

> Oh, 'tisn't manly, of course, 'tisn't manly, this method of wooing;
> 'Tisn't the way very likely to win. For the woman, they tell you,
> Ever prefers the audacious, the wilful, the vehement hero;
> She has no heart for the timid, the sensitive soul; and for knowledge.[6]

Moreover, the development of the dramatic monologue precisely in that historical moment when interest peaks in the fascinations of personality and in psychology as a discipline is also very suggestive. For Eliot, however, the dramatic monologue is no longer a vehicle for the exposure of an interesting personality, but an invitation to the reader to experience the dismantling of personality. The monologue invites the reader not simply to observe, but to participate actively in the poet's creation, from the inside as it were, by reenacting subjectively the world of the persona.

It was the critic Robert Langbaum who formulated the central rhetorical tension in the dramatic monologue, namely, "the effect created by the tension between sympathy and moral judgement."[7] The conflict between "sympathy" and "moral judgement" occurs not in the poem itself but in the reader. The tension we feel in reading Robert Browning's "My Last Duchess," for example, lies in our being charmed and delighted by the voice of an attractive personality while knowing, from his own lips, his capacity for barbarity and wickedness. The reader experiences an ambivalent response by which the speaker's wickedness somehow adds point and flavor to his charm. Of course, it is Browning who is responsible for creating this internal tension in the reader. Browning knew his readers better than they knew themselves. He knew the tremendous psychic charge which the exquisite joining in a single personality of the aesthete and the murderer might have on the moral sensibilities of mid-Victorian readers. The creation of a mask or persona, in which the poet disappears, so to speak, and tells his story in the guise of another character, offered Jules Laforgue and Eliot a way of viewing the narrator in what seemed to be an objective or ironic way. The persona can be simple or very elaborate, but it is always at a distance from both author and reader. Indeed, the poet seems to be in a relationship of collusion with the reader in watching and listening to this "character" out there.

Although we may judge a person or character on the basis of their behavior or morals, we may come to understand why they have done what they have done and as a result are drawn into possible sympathy. If they are wrongdoers or fundamentally dishonest or even amoral, our judgments are put into a state of tension with our sympathy for them as human beings. The dramatic monologue's power as poetry and, one supposes, its beauty, lies in just this tension. But we can take this one step further. The reader is always put in a position of taking in the persona in the poem in ways that the persona can never know or understand. This is very common in life. Others see you in ways that you can never know completely or surely; indeed, in all the intimacy of their perception you cannot control another's knowledge in its entirety, no matter what degree of personal disciplining of dress and manner you affect. There is always a gap between what or who you think you are and what or who others make of you. The dramatic monologue brings this gap or fissure to light. And Eliot's interest in this irresolvable dilemma tells us something, perhaps, of his psychology. At least, it can illuminate his literary critical interest in the poetry of impersonality. The need to invent personas and masks is tempered by the horror of how others might see us or might see past our façades, whether in judgment or sympathy, and, for Eliot, sympathy was the greater horror, even more than that of being judged. On one side of this divide lies abjection, abasement, humiliation; on the other, damnation. Eliot gave the name of J. Alfred Prufrock to this condition.

Laforgue led Eliot onto this terrain of poetry not only as an art but as a path to self-knowledge as well. Again and again Eliot would explore in his creative work the experience of abjection. In his poetry especially, he would open his speakers to the sickening dilemma and horror of contingency and the fraught tension between our own sense of self and the uncanny presence of others. The constant pressure of the unpredictable and our awareness of the limits of our knowledge in day-to-day life put into crisis the meaningfulness that gives to existence a semblance of stability. One can bring a great deal under personal control and give to it some kind of significance, but others are always sources of disruptive and disturbing power simply from their sheer presence out there beyond the reach of our knowledge. The other's presence marks the site where the relentless upwelling of the incalculable always threatens to undercut us. Our reaction to this varies only by the degrees to which the resulting trauma erodes our sense of wellbeing. This experience, so characteristic of modernity, penetrates us in many different ways. It can make us passively abject, dangerously obsessive, depressed, even violent and suicidal. A corpse, for example, represents a particularly sickening limit and puts our own wretched materiality before us; so do other provocative symbols, such as suppurating wounds, waste matter, rotting garbage, sewage, and, as suggested by the theorist of these maladies of the soul, Julia Kristeva, so does something as trivial as the sticky membrane that forms on the surface of hot milk.[8] Beginning in his earliest poetry, Eliot worked through these psychological tropes of inner horror until he was able to find a resolution in the redemptive promise of Christian faith, a point of rest – "still point" would be his phrase – that he would acknowledge in his greatest poem, *Four Quartets* (1944). But in his early collections of poetry and in his masterpiece, *The Waste Land* (1922), Eliot would explore abjection, inner horror, and disgust in a way that would make a whole generation of young people, a generation mutilated by war, come to know his work as if it were their own personal experience. The dramatic monologue form helped him to accomplish this.

"The Love Song of J. Alfred Prufrock" engages the reader's inner life by involving us in Prufrock's agonies, so that they become our own in the course of the poem. Eliot assembles an array of possible identities: the neurasthenic dandy for one (suggested by the stylistic proximity of Laforgue), the finally and truly damned (Guido de Montefeltro in the epigraph), Hesiod, Michelangelo, John the Baptist, Lazarus, Andrew Marvell, Hamlet, Polonius, and John Donne. The "Prufrock" voice urges us to test these choices of role in a state of nervy passivity. The point of view is only partially psychological here, though many critics and scholars read Prufrock's problems as entirely psychological. The hell that Prufrock occupies – Guido's speech from Dante's *Inferno* in the epigraph offers the first clue – is interpreted psychologically as something like a severe social phobia. If we return for a moment to Eliot's diagnosis of Byron, "a self that is largely a *deliberate* fabrication – a fabrication that is only completed in the *actual writing of the lines*" (my italics) – we can see that the issue cannot be entirely grasped in psychological terms. There is deliberation here and the process is not completed by the "self" in performance, as some form of life theatre, but is "completed" in language, "in the actual writing of the lines." Prufrock's problem is not a bad case of self-consciousness but a more deeply philosophical dilemma. The rattling play of self-images and the increasing awareness of personal identity as a metaphysical fiction unsettle both Prufrock and the reader. What has broken down in the poem is the editorial process by which we fabricate our identities.

By editorial process, I mean the cutting and pasting from the given cultural resources that we draw on in putting our selves together, whether from literary works or popular culture. That this new paradigm of the self begins to resemble a collage points toward the more ambitious performance of the same process in *The Waste Land*. The method of composing by assembling fragments is a means for avoiding linearity, a beginning-middle-and-end narrative, with its suggestion of purposiveness and necessity. Experience and language have lost their unity and resilience. The poem comes to us precisely as an accumulation of pieces, in short, a collage. If anyone were to set "Prufrock" to music, it would have to be to the accompaniment of shattering glass. The method of composition and the portrait of the human subject in the poem mirror each other.

Prufrock is the name of the zone where the usually silent and hidden process of self-fashioning is not only made visible but shown in crisis. As a result, Prufrock's suspension of the inherited canon of given identities becomes the only possible style that emphasizes a discernible separation from the phallic idiocy of Anglo-American hero worship. The speaker wonders whether he can "force the moment to its crisis" with his female companion. But he cannot find the appropriate role. He is, as he alludes, no John the Baptist or some other charismatic figure. He is in fact abject through and through. "I have seen the moment of my greatness flicker, / And I have seen the eternal Footman hold my coat, and snicker, / And in short, I was afraid" (*CP* 16). The conventional psychosocial mastery of Victorian male style cannot survive many such moments. Corroborative evidence for this can be found in the contemporary writings of Eliot's Bloomsbury acquaintance, Lytton Strachey. In *Eminent Victorians* (1918) Strachey's persona as historian, an innocent searcher after truth, takes on a refreshingly feline plasticity in contrast to his depressingly rigid and obsessed masculine subjects.[9] His four portraits provide an ironic survey of male style among the Victorians – including, most comically, that virile proconsul of hygiene, Florence Nightingale.

If we look past what the poem offers as drama, the performance of the speaker's anxieties, we find that it makes us look past inherited conventions of being: the existence, as we have noted, of an unshakable identity, expressed as the mask of personality, or of the existence of a will to power, of clearly marked gender differences, of male authority, and so on. These, in traditional settings, often act to regulate behavior and self-knowledge. "Prufrock" opens a vista on the working of these conventions through the poem's system of displacements. This is expressed in a number of ways and it becomes Eliot's principal operating procedure throughout his career. It begins in "The Love Song of J. Alfred Prufrock" where something like disparagement is at work. But it is not limited to the disparagement of an individual character named Prufrock. It extends to ways of writing and to certain kinds of poetry. Hugh Kenner in *Invisible Poet* hears Tennyson mocked in the reverberations of

> In the room the women come and go
> Talking of Michelangelo (13)

and in

> I grow old . . . I grow old . . .
> I shall wear the bottoms of my trousers rolled.   (*CP* 17)

Kenner suggests that the lines both destroy and recreate an established poetic discourse. The early critics of modernism often interpreted these destructive maneuvers as discursive purgatives, that is, a way of revitalizing moribund literary traditions.[10]

There is also something more radical at work. It is not only certain surpassed forms of poetry that are questioned but language itself. "The lines don't stand in an assured, ironic relationship to Victorian mannerisms: deep down, they turn in on themselves, insecure, self-doubting. Their sounds and their sense slide apart. The mock-heroic disproportion within the language becomes the means of revealing a radical flaw."[11] Eliot interferes with the conventional processes of making poetry. Direct statements lose their straightforward character. Not "I have gone at dusk through narrow streets" but "*Shall I say*, I have gone at dusk through narrow streets . . . ?" (15, my italics). Uncertainties of expression bleed into uncertainties of action, "Should I, after tea and cakes and ices, / Have the strength to force the moment to its crisis?" (15–16). The imperative gesture at the beginning of the poem, "Let us go then you and I" (13), is immediately immobilized in the operating room simile. This method of composition raises an important structural potential in the poem that is not often noticed. Prufrock can say anything, he is faced with enormous possibility; but he cannot *say* anything that communicates decision or even meaning. In terms of the process of the poem, at any particular point Eliot could go anywhere, but nowhere is necessary, or right. The writing here has attenuated or lost its sense of direction or destination. The wandering in the streets (or on the beach at the end) tropes the unstitching of one of the usual necessities of expression, that this is speech with a mission. The line quoted above is only a possible sentence; its assertiveness is undercut by the continual self-questioning ("Shall I say . . .?"). We are left with a poem, but only one from among the many that might have been. The lyric's normally compelling trajectory of feeling or emotion decays on the terrain of the subjunctive.

It also silences or displaces the lover's lyricism, the love song of the title. Prufrock recognizes from afar the luminosity of lyrical song, "I have heard the mermaids singing, each to each" (17). The reference to Donne's song "Catch a falling star" evokes the tradition of lyrical intensity, a place where language is radiant and active, where human voices, Donne's in this case, have the capacity for achieving song. Prufrock can only caricature this kind of lyricism; indeed, he cannot believe that it can be addressed to him – "I do not think that they will sing to me" (17). Again and again the poem cites inner authority wryly in order to dash it to the ground, "I am no prophet – and here's no great matter" (16). The poem refuses to legitimate the human subject on the basis of simple lyric effusiveness. Shelley might be able to write in 1822

> The keen stars were twinkling
> And the fair moon was rising among them,
> Dear Jane!
> The guitar was tinkling
> But the notes were not sweet till you sung them
> Again.[12]

By 1917 this emotional confidence lies in ruins. "The Love Song of J. Alfred Prufrock" refuses at every point to reproduce the emotional satisfactions of the love song. The affective, perhaps libidinal, unity for which "Jane" stands in Shelley's poem has been replaced by the libidinal obsessiveness of the fetishist: "Arms that are braceleted and white and bare / (But in the lamplight, downed with light brown hair!)" (15). The displacement of a lyric paradigm eludes both the structural pull of traditional verse forms and the constraints of a problematic subjectivity. The particular sound-shape of lines such as "Do I dare / Disturb the universe?" (14) is controlled not by genre, mode, or prosodic requirements, nor by the needs imposed by a philosophical idea or theme in the usual sense, but by the accumulated anxiety that the preceding lines constitute as a comic derangement of the persona of the late Victorian man of action. His decisiveness, it turns out, is propped up by his costume: "My morning coat, my collar mounting firmly to the chin" (14), the word "firmly" capturing here an elusive irony whereby resolve hollowly becomes a function of gentlemanly scrupulousness of dress.

What the poem brings vividly to our ears is the stammering into which a certain privileged humanist discourse has degenerated by Eliot's time. Stripped of all its typical maneuvers or camouflage, the human subject is laid bare. The Renaissance ideal of "Man" as the measure of all things has shrivelled to a "pair of ragged claws / Scuttling across the floors of silent seas" (15). Yet the sympathy we are asked to feel is not for the existential agonies of "modern man" hoping to have a heart-to-heart conversation in a world of chit-chat, but something more important than that. The poem silently laments the absence of an external or historical measure or standard for human agency, a criterion embodied in institutions (such as a church, for example) that give individual identities not only metaphysical density but meaning as well. What I mean by this is simply that we cannot ascend from the details of experience in "Prufrock" to a framing cosmology, as we can, say, in any of Donne's dramatic lyrics. "The Canonization" is an instance, no matter what mutations of tone the speaker performs, of the imperturbability of the Christian cosmos, not just as doctrine, but as a web of living norms, a model of thought, feeling, and conduct. The speaker's defiance in defence of a singular love at the beginning of Donne's poem, in which, at first, separation from the world is emphasized, slowly dissolves as he finds his way back under the symbolic canopy of Christian values from which, he discovers, the lovers have never really escaped. The changing tonalities of the speaking voice signal the phases of this motion without movement. Donne begins with an angry outburst which protects the libidinal integrity of the lovers. It ends in the celebratory calm of their inclusion through the ageless rituals of a historical community of feeling and belief.

"The Hollow Men"

The Prufrock world is revisited in "The Hollow Men" (*CP* 89–92). Although it is a poem about the dilemmas of belief, "The Hollow Men" is also explicit about language. Whatever it is that has happened to them – loss of faith, loss of belief in themselves – their voices have dried up and been made "quiet and meaningless" (89). In the "broken jaw of our lost kingdom," they "avoid speech" (91). The language of the poem lapses into the familiar sounds of childhood nursery rhymes (as near the end of *The Waste Land*) and yet they are strangely menacing. We are not surprised when it concludes in a defeated stammer:

> For Thine is
> Life is
> For Thine is the   (92)

The "Shadow" may fall across philosophical abstractions, "the idea / And the reality" (91–92), but it also falls across voices, halting them and turning them into whimpers, at the world's end (92). This is not all. The speaker in "The Hollow Men" does perceive a living language elsewhere, somewhere else, over "there," where

. . . voices are
In the wind's singing
More distant and more solemn
Than a fading star.   (90)

"There," language is singing and "voices *are*" (my italics). This distant lyricism cannot be heard in "the dead land" and neither can the "eyes" open wide on a visionary moment, "Sunlight on a broken column" (90). In anticipation of affirmations to come later in the 1920s, the speaker in the poem acknowledges "hope" (91) as he trembles "with tenderness" and yearns for lips that would "kiss" and "Form prayers" (91), the modal "would" here deferring faith, suspending belief, for the time being. But for now, in the moment of extreme doubt, the lines that ask "Is it like this / In death's other kingdom" (90) seem to render the visionary moment still more remote as the speaker considers the thoroughly distressing prospect that even "There," no redemptive vision is possible. The depths of this despair cannot yet be plumbed. He recoils, and in Section IV he returns to the experiential realities of life in "the hollow valley" (91), enumerating those things of which he is sure, painful and unsatisfying as they are. Subsequently, *Ash-Wednesday*, "Journey of the Magi," *Four Quartets*, and a series of verse plays would return to the themes of faith and belief. But before the religious turn, Eliot would have to continue the journey through hell begun with "The Love Song of J. Alfred Prufrock."

"Gerontion"

In 1920 Eliot published a slim volume of verse, *Poems 1920*, in which his scrutiny of the conditions besetting Prufrock and the hollow men are explored with a new incisiveness. The first and most important poem in the collection, "Gerontion" (*CP* 39–41), zeros in on themes only partially realized earlier. The dramatic monologue as a poetic form continues to be of use. We hear a new voice speaking, Gerontion, but there is very little to speak of, if we are looking to psychoanalyze him. He really is only a voice and a name, the name merely a rhetorical convenience or at least a way of conveying an aging subject, a man at the end of his life, and perhaps, a man, more forebodingly, at the end of his tether. Language is again a central concern, but now the references to it converge with a new vocabulary, the sermons of Lancelot Andrewes, a seventeenth-century clergyman whom Eliot had recently begun to read, and the Bible, the word already resonant of the Word. Eight years later, *Ash-Wednesday* will bring these associations into more secure alignment.

"Gerontion," however, brings to the surface a submerged theme in "The Love Song of J. Alfred Prufrock," namely, the status and value of the knowledge we gain from experience. The epigraph from Shakespeare's *Measure for Measure* (lll.i. 32–34) casts doubt on the value of experience when the speaker in the play, in this case the Duke, tells a condemned man that life is not worth keeping because one never has it in reality but merely experiences it as if it were a dream. In the philosophy of the modern age, from René Descartes to our own time, experience is the foundation of our knowledge. This is the basis of the scientific culture of the West and of its principal method of inquiry, the empirical imperative. What we can see, touch, hear, measure, weigh, and so forth, forms the ground on which we build the house of knowledge. Such a theory presupposes an observing subject of some philosophical substance, secure in his or her identity, secure in the validity and comprehensiveness of personal experience. After "Prufrock," such assumptions are at best dubious; at worst, if we begin to see through Eliot's eyes, they are a self-inflicted blindness that obscures true knowledge from our eyes. Gerontion has arrived at a place where experience will be held up for scrutiny like a lab specimen but minus the ruling illusions about its validity. Decay, deracination, delusion, disease are the conditions in which a "Blistered" and "peeled" humanity endures. On the horizon a menacing figure of retribution or redemption seems ready to spring. The modal grammar – "We would see a sign!" (39) – defers his coming, but we cannot be sure whether this could be put in Prufrock's idiom – "*Should I say*, we would see a sign" – or whether the modal now indicates unremitting spiritual distress.

We are offered characters to ponder, persons of uncertain race and lineage, but they prove to be fragments, merest apparitions. They are "Vacant shuttles" weaving the wind (40). Whatever they experience – aestheticism (Mr. Silvero and Hakagawa), the occult (Madame de Tornquist), madness or, perhaps, depravity (Fräulein von Kulp) – in the empty rituals they perform, they are trapped, like Gerontion himself, in a knowledge that is, at best, phantasmal. History, on the other hand, seems to offer a more durable form of knowing. But it, too, is "cunning," full of deception. The knowledge that history gives, in the form of its ruling muse, Clio, promises so much but merely leads to continuous confusion. In our hunger for knowledge, history leaves us more famished than ever. Knowledge is also belated, our "passion" is lost in the having and is only regained in some lesser form in "memory," as reconsidered passion. We think in history, that is to say, in time, but our confidence in it is shaken, because "what's thought can be dispensed with" (40) if it is only in history and only human.

Only when the "tiger springs in the new year" and we are devoured do we "Think at last" in a way that breaks the mold of old forms of knowledge. Gerontion confesses that he has lost his passion (41), but instead of seeing this as the close of life, the inevitable decay of our senses and of our capacity for experience, he sees it in a new light.

> I have lost my passion: why should I need to keep it
> Since what is kept must be adulterated?

The radical nature of this and the next two lines have rarely been appreciated in Eliot criticism. Gerontion is saying that passion is precisely what under-mines knowing – those things that we hold on to in life are adulterated things, adulterated inherently. Some readers hear these lines as saying that, as we age, the things of this life, such as passion, become adulterated as time goes on. With experience, we lose our innocence. Eliot is far more radical than this. We are born adulterated beings and remain so until we arrive on the other side of experience. Passion, rooted in the senses – "sight, smell, hearing, taste and touch" and, as a result, in a passionate self – seems to be the very thing that impedes us in our contact with reality or the truth of our being. Intellectual and emotional decisiveness can come only when we dispense with the passionate self. Gerontion asks, "How should I use them for your closer contact?" (41) and the answer is that the senses cannot be so used. Indeed, they are themselves the impediment and, worse, they are in our nature, not out there, somewhere, to be avoided.

The senses set off a kind of addictive "delirium." As we age, we try to excite them as they cool by the application of "pungent sauces" and the multipli-cation of variety. The catchphrase "variety is the spice of life," takes on a new, more sinister, meaning in this context. The senses lead us only into the wilderness, not the wilderness from which Christ the Tiger might spring – the voice from the desert – but into the "wilderness of mirrors" – a wilder-ness of self-deception, hallucination, and depravity. Against all this negativ-ity, the poem does manage to risk a moment of lyrical beauty, in the mood, perhaps, of regret, or resignation. The images are ravishing, but we are left with an inkling, not yet a statement, that even this stark beauty may prove in the end to be an obstacle to spiritual advance.

> Gull against the wind, in the windy straits
> Of Belle Isle, or running on the Horn.
> White feathers in the snow, . . .   (41)

For Eliot the poet, as opposed to Eliot the suffering consciousness, moments of exquisite lyricism are still alluring, even perhaps possessing redemptive possibilities. The charisma of exalted vision cannot be so easily dispensed with. In the early poetry these moments are treasured, but as he matures his understanding of them changes accordingly.

"Gerontion" was at one time destined to be part of *The Waste Land* but Eliot could not bring it into line with his plan for the longer poem. It appeared as the first poem in *Poems 1920* as a result of the association between Eliot and his American compatriot Ezra Pound. In this period, at the end of the First World War, the Eliot-Pound collaboration was at its most intense. It resulted most famously in the final version of *The Waste Land*, but also led them to begin composing in metrical and stanzaic forms as a protest against what they took to be the profligacy into which the new technique of free verse, or *vers libre*, had descended. Pound produced one of his greatest poems, *Hugh Selwyn Mauberley*, in 1920 as a result of this return to meter. It was a poem that was part memoir of the London avant-garde during the modernist decade between 1910 and 1920, and part a biting social satire of an England seen to be irredeemably uncouth and philistine.

Poems 1920

After "Gerontion," Eliot, too, trained a sardonic eye on the social scene around him and the characters and institutions to be found there in *Poems 1920*. The cast of characters he assembled in these poems were a cross-section of social types that Eliot saw as undermining the foundations of a social and political order held together by established values. It was liberal humanism, by exalting the individual above all else, that opened the gate for the arrival of the low and vulgar on the historical stage. The outsiders and the low – Burbank, Bleistein, Sweeney, Doris, Grishkin, Sir Alfred Mond – are all summarized in "A Cooking Egg" as the "red-eyed scavengers" who "are creeping / From Kentish Town to Golder's Green" (*CP* 47). But it is the next two lines, as question and answer, that set the satire against a deep nostalgia for imperial values:

> Where are the eagles and the trumpets?
> Buried beneath some snow-deep Alps.

Perhaps it was the shock of war, the radical changes in society, and the new political visibility of the lower classes and other marginalized groups that provided these lines with their undercurrent of disgust. Yet there was something deeper perhaps, something approaching a terribly unnerving abjection, a recoil of horror from contact with abject materiality, death-in-life, a breakdown of meaning, or a collapse of the distinction we make between self and other. The energy of disgust that flows through these poems is disturbing and has elicited some of the most spirited debate about Eliot's poetry.

That some of the names Eliot has chosen to include can be identified as Jewish and that Golder's Green is a suburb in north London with a large Jewish population opened the door on a long debate in Eliot criticism on the question of his anti-Semitism. This is not an easy matter to address and the debate has been fiercely vivid over the past few decades. It is probably not sufficient to argue that in these poems a rather larger cross-section of society is vilified than simply the Jews. If we include the poems written in French in the collection, Eliot seems to have cast quite a wide net of loathing, which ensnared characters from the Irish-sounding Sweeney to the rebarbative Americans (from Terre Haute, Indiana) in "Lune de Miel" (*CP* 50), and from the Russian Grishkin to the German philosopher in "Mélange Adultère de Tout" (*CP* 49), to name but a few. But there is no gainsaying that Eliot assigns the Jews a special place in his jaundiced survey. "The Jew," he writes in "Burbank with a Baedeker: Bleistein with a Cigar," "is underneath the lot" (*CP* 43). This is inexcusable, even though it would probably not have surprised very many contemporary readers in 1920. Our sense of its inappropriateness has been sharpened by the subsequent destruction of European Jewry by the Nazis and the knowledge that the incidental prejudice one hears in such comments contributed to an atmosphere of hatred that turned murderous in the 1930s. Yet, reading *Poems 1920* as a whole, we are left with a sense that there is a wider antipathy at work, much wider and more complex than the straightforward anti-Semitism of which Eliot now stands accused. He seems to be expressing disgust with humanity as a whole, primarily on religious grounds and over a wider territory than places where one might find Jewish people. The geography of these poems is global, from Antwerp (*CP* 39) to the "côtes brûlantes de Mozambique" (49), from the River Plate (59) to "Byzance" (50) and beyond. If the metaphysical crisis in "Gerontion" is a general condition, it extends its influence everywhere and over everyone, including over the one institution, the Church, where one might have other expectations.

> Flesh and blood is weak and frail.
> Susceptible to nervous shock;
> While the True Church can never fail
> For it is based upon a rock.   ("The Hippopotamus," *CP* 51)

Yet the "True Church" has also been debased. It is compared to a hippopotamus and the description of the Church – specifically the Church of England – as bloated, slumbering, blasphemous, and miasmic (51 – 52) does not leave much doubt as to Eliot's judgment. This opinion would change with time.

A more troubling matter at this period was the fact that Eliot consistently saw people in the worst possible terms, often as subhumans or nonhumans. A survey of *Poems 1920*, for example, reveals unrelenting abhorrence of humanity in general. Jews, for instance, are "spawned" (*CP* 39) rather than born, and when they are not squatting on window sills (39), they are reduced to "protozoic slime" (42) or symbolized as "rats" (43); the working class are referred to as orang-outangs (44), epileptics (45), "red-eyed scavengers" (47), "punaises" (50); people sometimes give off "une forte odeur chienne" (50) or "a feline smell" (56); they are always "en sueur" (49, 50) and silent vertebrates (59). There is no moment in Eliot's life as a poet where the abject is more fully in view than at this time. The nausea induced by these images of a diminished humanity leads Eliot directly into the intellectual and emotional terrain of *The Waste Land*. Kristeva in *The Powers of Horror* identifies this condition with the sudden apprehension of the materiality of existence, a materiality without God (*Powers* 4). It forces us to confront our own mortality, even our own death. The experience can be traumatic and encounters with the body, bodily fluids, or the bodies of others can induce abjection. The experience here is with the materiality of death, not with death as a concept, either through knowing about death or understanding what it might mean in a symbolic context. Kristeva puts it well:

> A wound with blood and pus, or the sickly, acrid smell of sweat, of decay, does not signify death. In the presence of signified death – a flat encephalograph, for instance – I would understand, react, or accept. No, as in true theater, without makeup or masks, refuse and corpses show me what I permanently thrust aside in order to live. These body fluids, this defilement, this shit are what life withstands, hardly and with difficulty, on the part of death. There, I am at the border of my condition as a living being.   (3)

This very border is reached again and again in *Poems 1920*, but nowhere more traumatically than in the last poem, "Sweeney Among the Nightingales" (*CP* 59–60), where blood, shit, and death provide the sequence with its culminating tableau at the end of the poem (60). The corpse of the dead king lies dishonored by the droppings of the singing birds (ironically nightingales, the sweetest singers of all), and we are left with an image of abjection from which we cannot avert our eyes. It has been anticipated in the poem's Greek epigraph from Aeschylus' *Agamemnon* when the dying king, struck down by Clytemnestra, cries out, "Alas, I have been struck a mortal blow." The opening image of "Apeneck Sweeney" and the melodramatic and faintly comical sexual encounter with a woman who "yawns and draws a stocking up" sets the stage for Agamemnon's death and the final descent into horror. No doubt there are some personal reasons for this encounter with the abject. We know that Eliot's marriage in the late 1910s and early 1920s was extremely unhappy. Temperamental differences were no doubt important in driving the couple apart. What held them together, however, was Vivien's constant need for medical attention. Her various physical ailments (including problems with menstruation), as well as emotional and mental collapses, kept Eliot by her bedside trying to nurse her back to health. But this biographical information does not explain the meaning of these images and of the atmosphere of revulsion and abjection that suffuses *Poems 1920*.

The Waste Land

In the early 1920s Eliot endured intellectual and spiritual crises as well as the personal dilemma he faced in his marriage. Intellect, spirit, and personal experience cannot, and could not in his case, be neatly separated. They combined dread, desire, abjection, and depression in a single tangle of thought and feeling. The philosopher might come to understand the crisis in terms of ideas but miss the passion; only the poet can convey the experience whole. After a long period of struggle with drafts of a text, collaboration with Pound, revision, and a nervous ailment that sent him to Switzerland at a crucial moment in the compositional process, Eliot was able to find a way of expressing this complicated state of mind and feeling. It took the form of his most celebrated poem, *The Waste Land* (*CP* 61–86).

The poem illustrated rather well one of Eliot's most important critical concepts, the "objective correlative," about which he had written in his essay on Shakespeare, "Hamlet and his Problems," in *The Sacred Wood* (1920). In the course of his analysis of *Hamlet*, Eliot advances a theory of how works of art convey not just ideas or themes but the full breadth and textures of experience. As we saw earlier, Eliot calls this procedure an "objective conclative," and if we examine his definition again (see page 34) we are reminded of the important roles that emotion and experience play in the effectiveness of a work of art. Notice that the materials that combine to yield what he calls a "formula" are carefully delineated as "a set of objects, a situation, a chain of events." Notice that he does not necessarily require a discernible narrative plot with characters, in appropriate settings, for the making of the work. He does not say they are completely unnecessary, but the phrase "a chain of events" is carefully chosen so as not to exclude other forms of combination of elements than traditional narrative ones. That he also allows for "a set of objects" and "a situation" to be equally important as elements in the work opens the text to wider formal possibilities than was the case in the past. Get the elements of the work in the right order, and the implication is that each work will have its own unique patterning and the whole experience from which the work emerges, will be "immediately evoked." Immediately is the key term in this phrase. What it implies is that no matter what ratiocinative sophistication one might bring to one's reading, the perfectly constructed work will have an impact that is immediate, whole, and certain.

All this seems easy enough in theory. The struggle actually to find the complete objective correlative among many objects or images, situations, and chains of events is far more difficult than the facile exposition of the idea can convey. Indeed, Eliot's struggles to give his materials the appropriate order to capture both a sense of time and place and his own personal dilemmas – intellectual, emotional, and spiritual – proved it to be very elusive. Firstly, one ought to acknowledge that *The Waste Land* is a text of the First World War and its aftermath. But it is a work that not only reflects the spirit of the times, it is a very personal document as well. With the end of the First World War, Eliot's financial and domestic situations had not changed. Worries over money, his wife's abdominal and gynecological disorders, her increasingly fragile mental state, and his own feelings of nervous exhaustion fed a growing sense of despair. The immediate postwar situation in Britain and Europe added to the sense of collapse and chaos. The disorder in Europe was particularly upsetting. He was aware of the situation in Central and Eastern Europe through his work for Lloyds. The collapse of the Prussian monarchy and Austro-Hungarian Empire, and the revolution in Russia, had led to further wars, insurrections, and various putsches and coups d'état in the small states that had replaced the imperial governments of the eastern monarchies. In England and France unstable governments and uncertain policies had led to rising unemployment and a general sense of drift when decisive leadership was needed. But most unsettling of all was the peace conference in Paris in 1919 at the old palace of Versailles, that other "wilderness of mirrors" that he seemed to have in mind when meditating on history in "Gerontion." The Treaty of Paris brought the hostilities to an end, but it also brought bitterness, acrimony, and desperation. The victorious powers used their advantage to exact a harsh revenge on their former enemies. Instead of reconciliation, the Treaty laid the foundation for conflicts to come, including setting in place one of the conditions that would lead to a new and more terrible war in 1939.

The Waste Land, born in a chaotic time, attempts to integrate a sense of fragmentation and disorder into its very texture. Indeed, the manuscript version of the poem that Eliot showed Pound in Paris only emphasizes this. By suggesting materials that could be excised, Pound helped Eliot to discover the crucial pillars on which the poem's integrity rests. It is perhaps too easy to reduce the poem's complexity and sophistication by trying to identify a single key to its meaning. The key to the poem may lie, paradoxically, in the fact that there is no single key to its meaning. Indeed, the poem needs to be read in a way that was unfamiliar to many contemporary readers of poetry in 1922 and still challenges readers today. The through-form of narrative or poetic plot seems to be missing, though many early readers found a convenient plot structure – the quest narrative – to grab on to. The poem's incidental reliance on medieval legends of the Holy Grail and the quest thereof pointed early readers and critics to a possibly coherent story in the text. But Eliot's appropriation of many different cultural resources, including ones from non-European sources, have always disturbed the composure of that explanation.

The dead king at the end of "Sweeney Among the Nightingales" and the sexual experience recounted in one of the French poems in *Poems 1920*, "Dans le Restaurant" (*CP* 53–54) help to identify two of the most important elements in *The Waste Land*. In this sense *Poems 1920*, and especially these two poems, are directly related to *The Waste Land* as a kind of overture in terms of theme, setting, and atmosphere. The dead or wounded king, whose infirmity has rendered the land waste, and the final lines of the French poem, which are reworked as the fourth section of the longer poem, suggest the creative proximity of the two earlier texts. Death and sex are the twin poles around which the diverse materials of *The Waste Land* are patterned, like iron filings fanning out from the two poles of a magnet.

Let us look first at the figure of the dead or wounded king; in *The Waste Land* wounded rather than dead though the dead or waste land in the Grail legend results from a possibly deadly infirmity of the king. It will be well in this context to remember the encounter with the abject already discussed. The corpse, of which there are more than one in the poem, and the wound are central images in making the concept of abjection a way of understanding the poem's moods and the demeanor of its characters. Eliot had already begun to work on the fragments that were eventually pulled together in his collaboration with Pound when he acquired a copy of Jessie L. Weston's *From Ritual to Romance* (1920), a book that traced the bundle of stories about the quest for the Holy Grail from earliest times to the European Middle Ages.[13] Weston's intent was partly scholarly, to bring to light the wealth of narrative materials relating to this important theme in European culture, and partly occult. Her work belongs to a widespread interest at the time in the occult and the wisdom literature on which it was based. The scholar Leon Surette has explored this fascinating episode in late nineteenth- and early twentieth-century European culture in *The Birth of Modernism*.[14] What began as pagan fertility rituals in ancient Greece and the Near East, Weston argued, evolved over centuries into the narrative romances that tell of the quest for the Grail, tales such as Wolfram van Eschenbach's *Parzival* cycle or Geoffrey of Monmouth's *Prophetia Merlini* in England, both texts of the twelfth century. Eliot's intent in this movement from ritual practices to narrative legends is, in a sense, to put the process in reverse; that is, to find within the legendary materials that have come to us as fiction their original basis in religious ritual – in other words, to reconstitute their most ancient core. The intent, in the contemporary setting, is to revitalize a moribund society and culture. In post-First World War Europe, it was not difficult to assert that European civilization and values were at a very low ebb.

Here it is necessary to consider for a moment Eliot's conception of society as it began to form from his Harvard days when he first encountered the discipline of anthropology. His thinking developed around the notion of a hierarchical society that achieves a kind of steady state or equilibrium, producing harmony at all levels: the symbolic order, institutional structures and practices, individual psychology, and concord in the means of expression. This ideal (and ancient) conception of society had, since the Renaissance, lost its cogency in a Europe that was growing increasingly secular, materialistic, and egalitarian, in which social change had descended into the arena of politics. Change was being driven by increasingly ungovernable forces, the dynamism of an increasingly unregulated market economy, the social fragmentation of ancient communities by the industrial scourge, the replacement of traditional wisdoms with expertise and democratic decision-making, and the rise of an ethics of individualism.

Eliot's sense of this great harmony was elaborated in the 1930s in *The Idea of Christian Society* (1939) and it was put forward as a criticism of the purely political conception of society.

> Thus, what I mean by a political philosophy is not merely even the conscious formulation of the ideal aims of a people, but the substratum of collective temperament, ways of behaviour and unconscious values which provides the material for the formulation. What we are seeking is not a programme for a party, but a way of life for a people: it is this which totalitarianism [he has Italian fascism and German national socialism principally in mind] has sought partly to revive, and partly to impose by force upon its peoples. (*Idea* 18)

We ought to notice that the customary character of a "way of life" is made incontestable by grounding it in "collective temperament," not in the region of politics, where ways of life become products of historical processes and are shaped by the volatilities of conflict and struggle. The core of ancient values, it should also be noted, agrees rather nicely with the idea of a collective temperament beyond the reach of politics.

Coordination and coherence of a type that Eliot might find comfortable were not salient features of the thoroughly dissonant, ceaselessly dynamic capitalist societies of the twentieth century. All societies, he felt, have an ideal form (an Idea in the Platonic sense) grounded in the "facts" of human nature and religion to which we should all resign ourselves. The contemporary world, with its emphasis on social progress, competition, individual freedom, and science, merely hid from view what is always embedded deeply, "the substratum of collective temperament." Societies in a healthy state display or express in their particular historical forms their proximity to the ideal. Societies that do not reflect it are entangled in a hallucinatory state of continuous and, ultimately, meaningless mutation. Nourished by their own nervous energies, such societies drown in the "hallucination of meaning" ("Swinburne as Poet," *SW* 149) inherited from the liberal humanism that had evolved as the dominant ideology of nations most fully pervaded by modernity.

After the catastrophe of the First World War, Eliot saw English society as living through a period when the reigning liberal humanism had "lost its cogency for behaviour," though it was still the only discourse "in which public speech [could] be framed" (*Idea* 20). But it was a discourse, Eliot argues, that had grown irredeemably incoherent. Everywhere, not only in the political arena but across the whole of life, it was reduced to stammers, charlatanism, and silence. This dismissal includes the humanist discourse of inwardness, what Eliot called, in "The Function of Criticism" in 1923, "the inner voice," or the voice of "Whiggery" (*SE* 18). "The Possessors" of this voice, he wrote, "ride ten in a compartment to a football match at Swansea, listening to the inner voice, which breathes the eternal message of vanity, fear, and lust" (*SE* 16).

The din of this corrupted inwardness is what we hear in a great many parts of *The Waste Land*. Madame Sosostris, the house agent's clerk, the typist, Sweeney, all express the same "eternal message." The exhausted despair of the Thames-daughters at the end of "The Fire Sermon" allows us to hear in the nihilism of the culminating word, "Nothing" (l. 305), the result of what for Eliot amounted to the swindle of Whig-liberal rhetoric. In the song of the Thames-daughters (ll. 266–306), two literary references stand out. Eliot himself draws attention to Richard Wagner's *Götterdämmerung* in his notes to the passage (*CP* 83). The second reference is to the Elizabethan court with the Queen and her lover, the Earl of Leicester, sailing the Thames during her reign in the late sixteenth century. The religious resonance of the phrase "humble people," like the allusions to Wagner and Elizabeth, functions as a sardonic diminution of the three singers and of the paltry inwardness that they express. The Thames-daughters are unable to position present experience in a wider, external context that transforms inwardness into something more vital and significant. The carefully chosen literary and religious allusions contrast with the so-called "lyricism" of "the inner voice." The optimistic humanist injunction to self-knowledge as the end of life leads, once the resources of mere personality have been spent, to nihilism. Our salvation, it seems, does not mean getting to know oneself better, but incorporation into a culture of custom and ceremony whose rooted orderliness and organic emotional life make sense of the inner chaos.

The sedated agonies of the Thames-daughters do not even belong to them. These are simply the exhaustions of an artificial inwardness that has finally collapsed. The quiet despair into which the women passively subside is as false as the sexual pleasure they want to continue to believe they have enjoyed. There is no salvation on the other side of degradation; there is simply more degradation. "Gerontion" ought to be our guide in these latitudes. Renewal for the Thames-daughters does not lie further inward toward some redemptive human essence but in escape from the suffocations of a merely human subjectivity. Trying to claim their "song" for a more hopeful view of human affairs is simply our embarrassment in the face of Eliot's punishingly severe attitudes toward the nameless Thames-daughters, laconically and remorsefully suffering sexual humiliation. Eliot was no humanist and we must beware of hoping against hope that he was.

In the end, their nerveless, flat songs falter on one word – "Nothing" – in a world that has lost its moorings. But even as their defunctive lyricism collapses into whimsical madness – "la la" – and silence, the ancient moorings are glimpsed again in the quotations from St. Augustine's *Confessions* and the Buddha's Fire Sermon (ll. 307–311). We are meant to register the contrasts and juxtapositions by which the text proceeds: the splendor of Elizabeth and Leicester regally sailing down the Thames set against the contemporary pollution of "The river sweats / Oil and tar," Wagner's *Rheintöchter* set against the Thames-daughters, the descent through lust to nihilism set against the purifications of Eastern and Western asceticism. Eliot's boldness in making his readers as uncomfortable as possible is perhaps no longer as well understood as it was in his day. He showed readers, comfortable in their humanism, a vision of their world from which the personal integrity of individuals, the redemptive potential of intimacy in personal relationships, free choice, and instrumental rationality have disappeared. He tried to show his readers that value, vitality, and, therefore, freedom lie in the proper sort of resignation to forces larger or deeper than ourselves, not in the endless entanglements of a freedom defined as the interminable exercise of personal will. If *The Waste Land* can be thought to have a "positive" message, it lies precisely in the strange negative strategy that aims to rescue us, or perhaps only Eliot himself in that moment of desperation, from anomie, personal despair, and a new freedom in a modernity that increasingly seemed meaningless. If the way back from all that meant the acceptance, for example, of cruelty, of blowing "the gaff on human nature" (*FLA* 51), and of a hundred other refusals to compromise the "belief in Divine Grace" (*SE* 17), then we should all have the courage, he felt, to stare the truth in the face, and not flinch.

This truth was not particularly difficult to discern or understand. After all, Christendom had believed it, fought over it, and even come to pay lip service to it for two millennia. The truth lay in what had come down to modern times as Christian orthodoxy. Some critics, such as Lyndall Gordon, have argued that Eliot's life and work together describe "a pattern of spiritual biography" moving from "a dead world to a new life" (*Early Eliot* 99). In support she quotes one of Eliot's London friends, Mary Hutchison, to the effect that *The Waste Land* was "Tom's autobiography" (86). Hindsight shows us that he was, in fact, moving toward an affirmation of Christian belief. What made this difficult was not the *need* to avow a faith – his need in the depths of a personal crisis is clear enough – but rather the sociological fact that commitment to a life of faith, a life in Christ in particular, had declined in an age of science, secularism, and sexual freedom. To be sure, Eliot believed, but he lived in a time when hardly anyone else did. The sacred texts of Christianity were still nominally venerated though they had lost, for many, their prestige as guides to knowledge and conduct since the Enlightenment.

Not the least important belief that Eliot came to hold was that of original sin (*FLA* 49). He certainly believed in this Christian metaphor of the human origin of ethical knowledge and, more surprisingly (some might say embarrassingly), believed in its relevance for the present day. Original sin contradicted, in all its spiky irreducibility, the meliorist optimism of liberal, utilitarian ethics which had displaced in the popular mind older Christian doctrines. This ethical progressivism had become the conventional account of moral and spiritual life in the nineteenth century. Not only were things getting better economically and politically, but ethical knowledge was improving in parallel. Original sin was the doctrinal fishbone on which the easy humanism of the time inevitably choked. It became the conservative vandal's handful of dust tossed in the gearbox of liberal optimism. It is clear that Eliot came to accept this old Christian doctrine very early in his life; it is already whirring away in the background to *The Waste Land*. The poem opens with what the poem knows already intact.

What the poem knows very clearly involves sexual experience and sexual guilt. "The Fire Sermon," especially in its final lines, "associates religious emotions with remorse for sexual wrong" (Gordon, *Early Eliot* 98). But the theme of sexuality, religion, and death permeates the whole poem, not just Part III. Weston makes it plain in *From Ritual to Romance* that the ritual practices of the past were deeply sexual, befitting their function as guarantors of fertility and the cyclical renewal of the land in spring. Sexuality is vitally connected with the cycle of renewal, the fertility of the land, and its ability to generate new life. In ancient myth and legend, a land's ecological fate is tied mystically to the health of the monarch, in this case the Fisher King, a central figure in Weston's book and the shadowy speaker at the end of the poem, "I sat upon the shore / Fishing, with the arid plain behind me" (ll. 423–424). The Fisher King is in a parlous state in the world of *The Waste Land*; his injury is sexual, rendering him impotent and unable to make the land fruitful. Only by the restoration of the king's health can the land be revived. The poem's title and its opening lines connect sex, death, and religion explicitly. The title of the first part, "The Burial of the Dead," taken from the Anglican Book of Common Prayer, points to the dead land and to the possibility of its revival in spring. But natural fertility is not an easy thing, is indeed labor, full of pain and longing. The social scenes sketched in the lines that follow bring the natural imagery into clearer focus. In a series of quick dissolves, now made familiar by film montage techniques, we are given fructifying rain, the sun ascendant, high mountains deep in snow, and a sense of freedom in a landscape gripped by winter. We hear several disparate voices: a Lithuanian German, a girl named Marie, whose words are taken from the courtier Marie Larisch's memoir of the Viennese court before the First World War, and a tourist in Munich sipping coffee by the Starnbergersee. The lake near the city is associated with another wounded king, Ludwig II (1845–86) of Bavaria, a patron of Wagner, and a man certified insane in the year of his suicide by drowning in the lake. Ludwig was a great lover of opera and art, but was tormented by his homosexuality and mental instability.

The desert imagery that follows adds a new religious dimension to what the poem has begun to create from the very start. Phrases from the books of Ezekiel and Ecclesiastes in the Old Testament sketch a desert landscape that comes to a sinister and personal focus in the line "I will show you fear in a

handful of dust" (l. 30). This is the lowest point physically and psychologically in the dead land. It is the moment of the most intense abjection. It is the
presence of the "shadow" in the previous lines that engenders the abject
subject in a new twist to the rational being produced by the old Cartesian
cogito; instead of "I think, therefore I am," we now have the abject subject as
the product of fear and all its associated terrors – horror, dread, panic,
depression. From this point in the poem, the mood of abjection ripples out
in concentric circles. Again and again, particular images – hanged men,
corpses, dogs, dirty ears, rats, skeletal bones, aborted fetuses, slime and
rubbish, wrinkled dugs and spilt semen, and so on to the end of the poem –
create a pattern that does not allow the abject human subject any relief.
Part V does gesture in the direction of a reconstituted subject, but it is a
project that ultimately fails.

Fear gives the mood of the poem its center of gravity. Fear is everywhere,
both in the said and in the unsaid. And in those filaments of feeling and
experience that cannot be said, because there is no language that can express
them. We hear it also in the poem's voices, and fear gathers like dead leaves in
a windy corner along the white spaces when the voices fail. It is part of
adolescent experience – "And when we were children / . . . I was frightened.
He said, Marie, / Marie, hold on tight. And down we went"(ll. 13–16) – and
it is the companion of the abject subject in adulthood – "Fear death by
water. / I see crowds of people, walking round in a ring" (ll. 55–56). We grow
so familiar with fear and trembling that we hardly notice how it shapes and
accents everything we feel, think, and do. It is the very air we breathe and like
the dry, dusty desert it chokes us. Fear is the shadow which rises to meet us
at evening (l. 29). It forces us into the arms of charlatans like Madame
Sosostris, the fortune-teller, the contemporary counterfeit of the prophetic
desert voices. It descends into the horror of Philomel's rape and mutilation
at the hands of the "the barbarous king" (l. 99) and it ascends to the key
of hysteria in the terror of the threatening, perhaps devouring, woman, in
"A Game of Chess,"

> Under the firelight, under the brush, her hair
> Spread out in fiery points
> Glowed into words, then would be savagely still.   (ll. 108–110).

It is fear that destroys the nerves of the middle-class wife, leading to the
dreadful wait for the monstrous revelation, death's "knock upon the door"
(l. 138). Fear pays no attention to wealth or class or education; it devastates
the aristocrat's stately home and penetrates the working-class pub, with
adultery and pain.

He's been in the army four years, he wants a good time,
And if you don't give it him, there's others will, I said.
Oh is there, she said. Something o' that, I said.
Then I'll know who to thank, she said, and give me a straight look.

(ll. 148–151)

And we hear it again as the pub fragment ends in the mad goodbyes of Ophelia. If *The Waste Land* were a piece of music, fear would be the dominant key to which each section returns again and again and again.

If fear keys the poem's mood as something we might ascribe to a person – say, the speaker in the poem – it is nonetheless a more general condition of the external world, inevitably embodied in the mood or atmosphere of post-First World War Europe. This mood is not simply the projection of a private state of mind onto the external world; it inheres in the external world itself. The sordid images of an obdurate reality – corpses, slimy river banks, red sullen faces – are objectively present, irreducible features of Otherness and our contact with them brings us to abjection as a condition of being, not simply as a personal state of mind. The trauma of the war, especially of the unprecedented suffering in the trenches, spread out from Flanders Field and all the other battlefields of the war across a Europe in shock. The devastation of the physical environment was bad enough, but it was moral and spiritual life that suffered more, to a degree from which there was no quick recovery. In many ways, the subsequent history of the West in the twentieth century has not brought back the old buoyancy of a failed innocence. We cannot return to a prior state after such knowledge. The Second World War would only confirm in more devastating detail what was glimpsed as a possible future on the banks of the River Somme in the summer of 1916. But fear is not simply a condition, a kind of dreadful atmosphere we must endure: it also enters the activities of the abject subject. The result is failure and failure is the major motif in the music of *The Waste Land*.

As we saw in Prufrock and some of Eliot's early lyrics, the abject subject can imagine, at a distance, moments of visionary intensity, but he cannot experience them himself. Prufrock knows that the mermaids will not sing to him. In "The Burial of the Dead," this moment arrives with the beautiful lines from Wagner's *Tristan und Isolde* I: 5–8 (ll. 31–34). As he accompanies Isolde on the long voyage to King Mark and Tristan, a sailor sings a melancholy song recalling his own love for an Irish maid. The voyage into the tragedy of unattainable love frames the most lyrical moment in *The Waste Land*. The hyacinth girl whose arms are full of flowers coming from the garden transfixes the speaker in the poem's principal epiphanic moment. But in the instant of vision, speech and sight fail and the abject subject is left stranded between life and death, between knowledge and oblivion. He looks into the "heart of light" and hears only "silence" (l. 41) In Western metaphysics "light" is traditionally the metaphor for the enlightened mind, the subject in full possession of knowledge. In this case, though, knowledge, too, fails. The silence to which the epiphany leads is claimed by the wider silence of *Tristan und Isolde*: "*Oed' und leer das Meer*," ("Waste and empty is the sea").

Yet failure is only the more obvious meaning of the passage. The word "silence" at the end of l. 41, we should note, corresponds to three negative expressions pointedly located at the end of the preceding three lines, "not" (l. 38), "neither" (l. 39), and "nothing" (l. 40). The emphasis that the line-breaks place on negation is deliberate. "Nothing" and "silence" are linked in the semantics of the poem's formal organization. They seem to be the marks of lyric failure and for all intents and purposes, that is, the purpose of aesthetic beauty and redemption through art, they are. But "nothing" and "silence" are, in another sense, affirmative expressions and point us in another direction. "I knew nothing" can mean knowing nothing as an actual knowledge of something, possibly the nothing that always lies on the other side of the material world. Silence, too, points, not to the absence of words or music, but to what lies beyond the reach of either. The other way of putting it, "I did not know anything" is the dead end of knowledge.

The poem offers up another avenue to negation in "A Game of Chess," but this time Eliot switches genres. Instead of private lyric we have a little chamber drama, a scene drawn from the countless private lives of married couples come to the end of their tether. The man in the passage "never speak[s]" (l. 112), so it is not exactly a dialogue. The man's responses to the woman's anxious questions remain in his head as she probes: "'Do / You know nothing? Do you see nothing? Do you remember / Nothing?'" (ll. 121–123). Her panicky talk returns six times to the word "nothing," and as with the repetition of any word over and over again, the repetitions begin to change its meanings and even its sound; "nothing" in this context takes on new resonances. In the design of the section, the affirmative meaning of "nothing" as something that might be known, seen, or even remembered is evoked by the unspeaking subject in a series of images of abjection, "rats' alley" (l. 115), the bones of dead men (l. 116), a drowned son remembered from Shakespeare's *The Tempest* (l. 125), and staring, "lidless" eyes (l. 138), climaxing with the trembling wait for death's knock "upon the door" (l. 138). But what does this door lead to? Nothing as annihilation? Or nothing as a luminosity beyond knowledge, sight, or memory? *The Waste Land* cannot answer this more general philosophical and religious question just yet. Eliot will himself have to move toward new affirmations in the years after *The Waste Land.* But the way seems already to have been marked out via the poem's many references to spiritual traditions.

In "The Burial of the Dead" we have heard prophetic voices, then they are joined in Part III by both Christian and Buddhist voices, then in Part V, "What the Thunder Said," by voices drawn from the Hindu *Vedas,* specifically the *Brihadaranyaka Upanishad.* The poem also resurrects the pre-Christian religions of the Eastern Mediterranean, especially the fertility religions of the ancient Greeks and the peoples of Asia Minor. Moreover, Eliot did not impose a temporal scheme on the evolution of these religious traditions, even though they have originated in different times and places. These traditions are primal, that is to say, fundamental to human consciousness and to the making of human communities. They are as relevant in the twentieth century as they were in the time of their emergence.

This sense of the continuous relevance of the past for the present was one of the cornerstones of Eliot's literary criticism in "Tradition and the Individual Talent" (1919). In that key critical text, he writes that "art never improves, but . . . the material of art is never quite the same" (*SW* 51). On the evidence of his poetry, we could say something very similar about Eliot's sense of the primordiality of a culture's religious traditions. And if we agree that the mind of one's culture "is more important" than one's own private mind, then the religious impulse is not simply a matter of individual faith or personal beliefs. Those beliefs constitute the reality for those through whom they speak. Renaissance and post-Renaissance liberal humanism and the Enlightenment traditions that have organized the intellectual life of the West have imposed a barrier between the Western mind and its more primal depths. In this spiritually uncommitted period in Eliot's life, he was not about to privilege one of these traditions over any others. Although grounded in European religions, there was no Christian or biblical provincialism in Eliot's spiritual explorations. This would change, of course, but not because he found Hindu and Buddhist beliefs wanting as opposed to his new Christian avowals. Having understood that the embrace of a faith was not a purely personal matter but contained important social and, indeed, political meanings and elements, he was not about to make of his faith an eclectic mixture of diverse materials stitched together from the attractive bits of each system. In *The Sacred Wood* he had compared William Blake, who had done just this, to Dante, who had not. Blake, great as he was, was nonetheless an "imperfect" poet precisely because he had cobbled together a mystical religion of his own. Dante, on the other hand, had brought to one of its highest expressions a religious tradition that was both deeply historical and deeply personal.

In *The Divine Comedy* the historical and the personal intersect to make Dante a model of the kind of perfection that a great poet ought to seek.

These thematic issues have the effect of leading us out beyond the boundaries of the poem to engagements with the intellectual currents of Eliot's day. The questions of religion, personal belief, new ideas of the self, new communal orders, and the political and historical crises into which Europe had slipped during the war period were dramatic and important topics. Eliot's eye was fixed on the contemporary world and there are many places in *The Waste Land* where we can note Eliot's reaction to the crises all around. The fall of the three empires in Central and Eastern Europe – the Prussian, the Austrian, and the Russian – are alluded to in several places. The decline of religion and the arrival of fortune-telling charlatans in its stead are the subject of satire in Part I. The loss of social cohesion as a result of secularism and the political arrival of working-class characters like "the young man carbuncular" communicate Eliot's sense of his own time. This is perhaps why, when the poem was first published, it was thought to be a work that expressed the disillusionment of a generation. *The Waste Land* certainly does that, but it does so only in part. The poem is more extreme than mere satire. It exemplifies a philosophical radicalism that goes to the heart of twentieth-century thought. In "Tradition and the Individual Talent" again, Eliot remarks that, in the essay, the "point of view he is struggling to attack is perhaps related to the metaphysical theory of the substantial unity of the soul" (*SW* 56). One can say of this statement that it has often been quoted but not sufficiently well understood. That it comes in the midst of an essay of literary criticism and theory is the first point to note. One might expect such a statement to be encountered in a philosophical or theological text. But here it is in this unexpected context. What does this sense of the soul as not substantially unified have to do with the creative process and with the works of art that are its products? It turns out that this is the point where the real drama of *The Waste Land* is to be found.

Oddly enough, the uncertain unity of the soul returns us to what lies at the core of Eliot's thought, the question of language. Eliot's philosophical studies, with their anthropological leanings, had brought the relationship between language and reality vividly to mind. How does language convey a sense of the real when it is patently a system of second-order symbols that impose abstract patterns and meanings on experience? These patterns and meanings do not necessarily inhere in reality; they are very likely systemic projections of the language system itself. The action "John throws the ball" does not happen and is not perceived as happening as a rapid concatenation of grammatical categories. Something primordial occurs to put us in contact with the event.

That primordiality cannot be entirely captured in language because language works via categorical and generic processes and the primordial does not. The absolute uniqueness and singularity of an event inevitably escapes the reach of language. Indeed, language acts to simplify the welter of impressions, experiences, and impingements of the real on consciousness (including the consciousness of the body). Without that screening process, or process of ordering sense impressions and experiences, we would be unable to control or manipulate our fields of living and would perhaps be subject, like the animals, to the shaping obligations of our nervous system. Unlike, say, cats or dogs that instinctively turn toward the sun on a warm day, human beings have the power to negate or resist the compulsions of our nerve endings and our bodies.

Language in its social uses acts to simplify and arrange. It gives us a repertoire of devices, vocabularies, and rules in order to regulate the endless flux or stream of experience. Most social uses of language capture and control, order and pattern experience and the knowledge that we gain from it. Only the creative artist, the poet, puts into question the received orderliness of social discourse. Only the poet, working within the limits imposed by language, manages at the same time to breach those limits. Language for the poet is both an instrument for the preservation of order and an instrument for its radical dishevelment. This may sound contradictory, but it is the poet's task to make the paradox work. We are not to think of these opposing intentions in the same way that we might think of the contest of two ideas, which either lead to a higher concept or are resolved in some other way. What I am describing is by its very nature irresolvable. The positive language of themes and satire, social and historical descriptions, are opposed not by other descriptions and explanations but by negation. Unlike the stability of the social text, wherein difference and disruption of meaning is moderated, the poetic text generates difference, sometimes enthusiastically, sometimes slyly. In short, it multiplies variance, ambiguity, and surprise. Disturbance and disruption of the smooth operation of social languages goes to the heart of its calling as poetry. One can argue, no doubt, that all texts generate difference as part of the internal character of language as such, but social texts work to stabilize or diminish the play of difference. Poems do not, or at least not to the same extent. Among other things, they draw attention to the anxiety of a radically ruptured text and *The Waste Land* is a highly anxious text.

The practice of narrative by luminous fragments was, in 1922, a new approach to the cohesiveness of a text. It both suggested possibly coherent sequences and, at the same, revealed the cleavages that continually interrupted the seamless flow of words. The effect of this procedure is to place all the fragments in quotation marks so to speak, to hold them at arm's length in a gesture of critical distancing. The mind of the poet composing takes on a critical cast in addition to the energies of creative inspiration. The poem, as a result, is a critical act as well as a creative one. The way in which the language and form of the poem constantly draw attention to their own status as communicative processes moves in two directions in *The Waste Land*.

In the first instance it blocks a reader's easy consumption of the text. The text is difficult. It resists the usual procedures of interpretation. Seeming to lack a semantic center of gravity that can be located in the text, the poem's references to a familiar external world – the seasons, familiar landscapes, familiar social settings and activities – suggest that its unity might lie outside its boundaries, out there in the world. This might suggest that the poem is primarily a satire, a way of looking askance at the failures of a moribund society. The mythological roots of the poem, then, might be interpreted as the scale of implicit values that all true satires must have in order to show how badly contemporary society fares in comparison. The vitality of ancient fertility rites belittles the sterile sexual fumblings of clerk and typist. But let me try to be a little more specific about how *The Waste Land* can function as a satiric text.

It is true that a poem never occurs in a social vacuum. It always bears the marks of the social world and bears also identifiable attitudes toward that world. An allusion to Chaucer, for example, is also an allusion to a particular conjunction of sociocultural meanings. "April is the cruellest month . . ." reminds us of Chaucer and his world, acting as an emblem of social and spiritual values. In the surprising context of *The Waste Land*, however, it is not Chaucer as such who is pulled into the poem but what "Chaucer" has come to signify. This new context rescues Chaucer from the clichés about the warm, comic poet laureate of a quaint, merry, old, orderly England, the first national poet in whom that superior native Englishness is discerned. Or so the narrative of nationhood makes plain, quietly working away inside a reader's head. This picture, originating primarily in the nineteenth century, denies the historical Chaucer's cosmopolitanism, the formation of his mind, not by a narrow provincialism, but by his contact with and respect for Latin, Catholic Europe. This is the Chaucer that Eliot brings into the poem.

The choice of "cruellest" is also deliberate, a challenge to the routine Romantic nature lyric being written in the late nineteenth century. The word swerves from the well-worn path of a debased Romantic poetic diction, which would make a line about spring beginning with "April" something sweet and sickly. Eliot's word gains its clarity and definition the moment a reader feels their way into the contrast that "cruellest" makes with the usual poeticized abstractions about spring. The lines in *The Waste Land* that follow (ll. 1–7) continue to cross terrain resisting their easy consumption as familiar nature poetry. They evoke pain and struggle, rather than the happy buzz of flora and fauna in spring. They question the prettified and petrified literary language – "Spring, dancing light-foot down the woodland ways" – of a Rupert Brooke.[15] One could multiply examples in the poem where Eliot's language challenges and rewrites the conventional poetic diction of late Victorian and Georgian poetry. *The Waste Land* does not exist in its own space, in a world of its own; it finds itself in the world already, but not innocently, not without, as they say, attitude.

But this concern with sociocultural context, what I am calling, for want of a better term, the satiric intent, is not the only direction in which the poem moves. The struggle to make the poem is not only literary or formal. There is more at stake with the risks that Eliot is taking. The whole thing threatens to collapse and, in fact, it was probably some sense of the unmanageability of all the materials that he had put in play that made Eliot seek Pound's help. If we return to the keys of "nothing" and "silence" that occur in what is the lyric heart of the poem, we can understand better the philosophical, even existential, drama which the poem enacts. Eliot's intellectual evolution is implicated in this compositional scene. Having been brought to the limits of both language and rationality, he sought to find a way of expressing the inexpressible. The use of fragments as the primary building blocks of the poem made it possible to glimpse into the "heart of silence" without being able to embody it in the usual language of poetry, namely metaphor and symbol. It might be easy to say that what he was seeking was the real, the real beyond the apparatuses of representation which language interposes between the mind and the external world. Reality, the real, cannot be perceived immediately. No sooner is it named than it is changed. This is a philosophical dilemma of which Eliot was very much aware as a graduate student at Harvard. As I have said before, it would be easy to pursue this line of inquiry. But this was not what Eliot was after. He was after a reality beyond the real, one that could anchor the emotional, intellectual, and moral life of the person. Some groundwork of values that would not shift with time.

The only intellectual tradition that could offer any way past the dilemma of social and moral relativity was, and perhaps still is, religion. "Nothing" and "silence" were the preliminary steps toward the wider and greater vision. *The Waste Land* represents the movement toward such a crossroads, but it does not bring the poet or the reader to the sought-after destination. Perhaps the pilgrim does not know the way to the shrine where life can be transformed. But he has heard rumors of its power to replenish life. Here the poem's peripatetic character comes into play. The speaker is not on a quest, as most critics have speculated; this is a pilgrimage. Unlike Chaucer's pilgrims, however, who know the destination (Canterbury) and the way, Eliot's pilgrim is unsure of the path to the holy place. And he is unsure that he will even be able to recognize it when he gets there. The journeying motif that runs through the poem is precisely the single most important structural device that Eliot uses. We move around London encountering all those images of waste and decay that bring us to abjection, but we cannot find the redemptive shrine. From London, we move to Carthage, to Phoenicia, to other cities of Europe, to the mountains, and eventually back to London Bridge and the Fisher King vowing to set his lands in order (l. 425). The shrine cannot be reached, not here and not yet.

In Part V we seem to be nearing the goal, but again the pilgrim is disappointed. The land is lying waste even as we ascend the mountains in the typical movement toward transcendence. The human world has not been able to deliver the promised satisfactions, emotional, intellectual, or sexual. The poem turns from human language to the languages of nature, animal for example, birdsong – of nightingale, hermit-thrush and cockerel – the whirr of the cicada, the drip of water, and, most promising of all, the crash of thunder. But what sense does the thunder make? It offers not a word, certainly not the Word, but a syllable, DA, the primal particle of all Indo-European languages. It comes from a language which does not exist, but from which all other languages have evolved. The primal syllable is elaborated in three Sanskrit injunctions, *Datta, Dayadhvam, Damyata,* translated as Give, Sympathize, Control. If this is the wisdom to be gained by winning the holy shrine of pilgrimage, it seems that we may have arrived at the sought-after place. But the words spoken by the thunder are glossed, and with each gloss we are returned to this side of revelation, only a partial understanding of what lies beyond language, experience, and knowledge. They speak of death, imprisonment, and obedience. On the poem's showing we can expect death and imprisonment. Obedience is the new term and the crucial one. It will shine out later in Eliot's work after his conversion to the Church. The poem ends with the repetition of the three injunctions and with the word "Shantih," the formal ending to an Upanishad, meaning the peace that surpasses all understanding.

The astonishing success of *The Waste Land* in the 1920s ironically also turned out to be a kind of failure. The poem enjoyed the worst possible kind of esteem. It became fashionable. It fell to the new hungers that an increasingly resourceful consumer society had stimulated, a society that in the cultural regions was just beginning to learn how to consume new styles of art and aesthetic shock effects. The taste for dissonance and Dada developed as the inward analogue to the volatilities and collisions of a perpetually overheating market economy. The poem was simply appropriated, that is to say, denatured and declawed, in a way that has become familiar in the culture industries of the West, whether it be *The Waste Land*, punk, or hip hop. It was made over for consumption as the most fashionable avant-garde cultural artefact in the 1920s. Certainly, Evelyn Waugh remembered the reception of the poem in those terms in *Brideshead Revisited* (1945).[16] In the famous balcony scene, the camp aesthete, Anthony Blanche, frivolously croons lines from the poem to crowds of Oxford students below.

The best that can be said for Eliot is that, as soon as he saw what was happening to his poem, he virtually disowned it. We can only speculate why. For one thing, he made a grave error in his estimation of the real vulnerabilities of his audience. As a still marginalized intellectual, he thought, rather quixotically, that everyone was as serious as he was. He also suffered the typical delusions of most solitary revolutionary outsiders, that the necessity and efficacy of the revolutionary poetic act would be as compelling in reception as we know it was for him in composition. *The Waste Land*, in this perspective, can be seen as an act of discursive terrorism. The bomb went off, but instead of changing hearts and minds, the poem contributed only a few more fashionable languors; contributed, as Eliot himself disgustedly recalled in 1931, merely, the "illusion of being disillusioned" (*SE* 324).

His misreading of his readers also led him to misunderstand the nature of his contemporaries' hunger for change. Everyone in the 1920s talked about the need for change and renewal. The First World War had accelerated that conversation. But what an intellectual like Eliot might mean by renewal was not exactly what the consuming masses seemed to mean by it. For the new era of consumption, remorseless and constant change became the inevitable framework of material life. The repeated exhilarations aroused by the continuous pursuit of the new, of the latest, of the most desirable, penetrated the psyche as deeply as it pervaded the ceaseless flow of goods. In the nineteenth century if a man changed or lost his religious faith, he spent the rest of his life living through the implications and consequences of the trauma. Even John Henry Newman's courageous but relatively simple change of ecclesiastical allegiance involved agonized self-examination and public apology for a lifetime. By the 1920s it was certainly still possible to write an *Apologia Pro Vita Sua*, but only if one could manage it in a month.

The Ariel poems and *Ash-Wednesday*

In the mid and late 1920s, as *The Waste Land* brought Eliot a measure of fame and notoriety, he was beginning to undergo the spiritual experience that would define the rest of his life both as a person and as a writer. *The Waste Land* was written by a man who seemed on the edge of a breakdown. In fact, Eliot had needed professional help during the composition and editorial process for ailments that were essentially emotional and psychological. Clearly, the disaster of his marriage had much to do with this. In these circumstances, the Church seemed to offer something – both an end to the emotional pain he felt and a new beginning. He explored the possibility of conversion in a new series of poems from 1925 on, culminating in his greatest work of this period, *Ash-Wednesday* (1930). As his friends, acquaintances, and even his new fans read these works, they were somewhat confused by what seemed a radically new direction which his previous works did not seem to anticipate. Only those closest to Eliot were aware of the spiritual struggle through which he was passing in the late 1920s. For others, it would have been difficult to understand the significance of *Ash-Wednesday* in Eliot's evolution as an artist.

The short dramatic monologues that were published as the Ariel poems – "Journey of the Magi," "A Song for Simeon," "Animula," and "Marina" – would have provided a clue, though as dramatic monologues it was difficult to say whether they were genuinely moving toward an affirmation of Christian faith or were further explorations of particular voices, personas, and beliefs without any commitment intended. If one were one of the Magi on the way home after the revelation at Bethlehem, how would one feel? Even a confirmed atheist could pose that question and imagine the journey back to his kingdom. Was *Ash-Wednesday* a genuinely Christian poem or was it one more elaborate persona in a life of sustained role-play? When word of Eliot's actual conversion to the Church of England became public knowledge, any doubts about his new allegiances vanished. He had made his decision and he was now following through in good faith. The Ariel poems set down the forwarding address, but it was *Ash-Wednesday* that sealed the envelope.

The hardest part of the process, for a highly sophisticated and educated man, was the rediscovery of a radical innocence in a fallen world. "Animula" descants on the theme of the "simple soul" (*CP* 113), ending with a child's prayer for the heroes of youth. The final line – "Pray for us now and at the hour of our birth" – wittily substitutes "birth" for "death" as found in the common prayer *Ora pro nobis* . . . "A Song for Simeon" looks at life from its nether end, that is, old age and the approach of death and the consolation possible in peace offered by the wonderful "Infant" and "the still unspeaking and unspoken Word" (*CP* 111). "Marina," composed in 1929, and closely related to *Ash-Wednesday,* allows us to hear a speaker (the allusion is to Shakespeare's Pericles in the play *Pericles, Prince of Tyre*) come to the moment of crisis and the confusion of identity and relationship that ensues as a result of a momentous transformation. At the beginning of the poem, Pericles seems unable to find a place or to know even where he is. The sense of confusion is sustained throughout the poem, culminating in its most important lines:

> I made this, I have forgotten
> And remember.
> . . .
> Made this unknowing, half conscious, unknown, my own.   (*CP* 116)

The twinned themes of memory and unknowing recollect the ideas of silence and nothing from *The Waste Land* and look forward to the mystical elements in *Four Quartets.* The kind of journey that the Christian pilgrim must undertake requires acceptance of what one has been and what one has done ("I have made this"), the need to put both of those aside ("I have forgotten") and to recall the necessaries of significant life ("And remember"). The gift that comes from faith cannot be gained by intellectual exertions alone. It requires a kind of unknowing, a forgetting and a remembering, being alert to what is half-consciously grasped and being able to go forward without any guarantees.

"Journey of the Magi," the greatest of the Ariel poems, clearly defines the dilemma faced by the new convert to faith, especially if one is a significant individual with public responsibilities. Here we have another pilgrimage but now to a more familiar place, Bethlehem, for the birth of the infant Christ. The Magus is a powerful man, king-like, weighed down by his obligations to his people. The journey there was difficult, it was after all the "dead of winter" and the territories through which he had to pass were "hostile" and "unfriendly" (*CP* 109). There were premonitions of things to come in the life of the infant Redeemer, but they lay in the future. It was the present moment and the even more difficult journey back to his kingdom that focus the Magus's mind at the end of the poem. Here we come closest to Eliot's own dilemma in becoming a professing Anglican. The encounter with the infant Christ transforms the Magus. It is not clear that he has fully understood the change of orientation and consciousness that occurs at the moment of "Finding the place" (110). But it is clear that this is a personal transformation in a world that has not yet experienced and is not aware of the transfiguring presence already on earth. The greatness of the poem lies in its capturing something of the alienated state in which the Magus now finds himself as a result of his radical transformation. The birth establishes a whole new order of meaning for one's life. These new circumstances make it extraordinarily difficult to return to "the old dispensation" (110) as if nothing has happened. The Magus is "no longer at ease" and cannot feel at home among "an alien people clutching their gods." This captures very well the awkwardness felt by the faithful among pagans or nonbelievers and vice versa. It speaks directly to Eliot's own dilemma in a modernity in which religious beliefs had declined in the population at large and among the intelligentsia. On the plane of redemption, there occurs the same process which Eliot says takes place on the plane of artistic creation – "For order to persist after the supervention of novelty, the whole existing order must be, if ever so slightly, altered" (*SW* 50). Life-altering changes cannot be ever so slight, but they do put one in a position of permanent exile. Indeed, the poem's concluding line affirms that the birth the Magus witnessed was necessarily a kind of death, death to an old life and rebirth in the new.

Eliot was not a poet who confessed to writing autobiographically at any time in his life. He never forwent the practice of impersonality in his poetry in order to speak in his own voice, even as he was undergoing the tectonic shift in religious sensibility that is so well enacted in *Ash-Wednesday*. Yet there are situations that he dramatizes in his poetry and plays which carry auto-biographical resonances. His recourse to the dramatic monologue made it possible to deflect more easily what he would have considered the wrong type of critical interest in his work. *Ash-Wednesday* is still based on a set of literary sources. In the first line we hear Guido Cavalcanti's "Perch'io non spero di tornar gia mai . . ."[17] as well as Lancelot Andrewes's Ash Wednesday sermon of 1619. However, the learning the poem wears is narrower and more local. It derives from mainly English and Anglican sources with the exception of the Italian *trecentisti*, poets from fourteenth-century Tuscany. There are references and allusions to Shakespeare's sonnets, the Anglican Book of Common Prayer, the Hymnal, the language of the Thirty-Nine Articles, the Anglo-Catholic Prayer Book, the Cavalier devotional tradition, and, of course, Dante. The poems that make up the *Ash-Wednesday* sequence speak with greater directness and simplicity than had been Eliot's practice in the past. His famous obscurity and difficulty was replaced by a straightforwardness that was meant, perhaps, to be disarming, to establish his *bona fides* in the matter of his new affiliations. Eliot better than anyone else understood that he had his own previous reputation for speaking in masks to overcome.

In devotional literature it is often the case that the culmination of the work comes in the form of a vision of God or of a moment of impregnation by and union with the divine. This is especially true of the seventeenth-century poetry and prose that Eliot was reading during the composition of *Ash-Wednesday*. Eliot's poem is devotional, to be sure, but it does not follow the typical pattern. There is no easy commerce with the otherworldly as in Henry Vaughan's "The World":

> I saw eternity the other night
> Like a great ring of pure and endless light, . . .[18]

Nor does the poet call out wantonly for God's punishing hand, "Batter my heart, three-personed God" as in John Donne's Sonnet 14.[19] Neither does Eliot indulge in Richard Crashaw's voluptuous and sexualized embrace of divine ecstasy, "What heaven-entreated heart is this, / Stands trembling at the gate of bliss" ("To the Noblest and Best of Ladyes, the Countesse of Denbigh).[20] *Ash-Wednesday*'s language is indebted to the reserve, humility, and economy of expression to be found in George Herbert, rather than in the more exhibitionistic performances of the late Donne and Crashaw. In fact, it was to Herbert that Eliot had increasingly turned since his early interest in the metaphysical poets had been stimulated by Donne's dramatic lyrics a decade earlier.

Moreover, Eliot's poem does not dramatize the encounter with the divine as the central matter of the poem. Rather, *Ash-Wednesday* must be seen as working out the tension between matter and spirit, between the sensuous and spiritual bodies. To some extent, the part of our being that is earthbound and takes in the world through our senses must be occupied by emotions, feelings, and ideas, by ritual and ceremony, in order to allow the spirit to contemplate and ascend through the agency of an intercessor, in this case the Lady, toward a glimpse of the divine in a timeless moment. This glimpse, or even potential union with God, does not occur in the poem but is conveyed by what the poem cannot yet say. What appears in the material text is movement toward what a mystical tradition might see as the appropriate annihilation of the sensuous body in order to release the ethereal spirit into the realm of God's light. But this is not Eliot's goal. Eliot is far more complex in his thinking; after all, the obliteration of the sensuous body endangers more than the calming of lust or other purely physical desires. It imperils the very art he has devoted his life to making. Eliot's goal is much more subtle. *Ash-Wednesday* pushes toward it, but he will not bring it entirely to light until *Four Quartets*. So what is "it" exactly?

The true mystery of the Christian faith lies in the concept of Incarnation, whereby the Spirit of God descends from its unearthly plane into the body of the world, into the body of a man, wherein Man and God are made one. Both *Ash-Wednesday* and *Four Quartets* explore this central Christian belief. It is, of course, a paradox, one that cannot be explained rationally. It can be brought to the light only by image and symbol, by invocations of nature and by their negation. The Incarnation defines the intersection of the human and the divine, the place where the body and spirit are not only joined but are made one. The title, *Ash-Wednesday*, refers to one of Christianity's holy days. In the Ash Wednesday Mass the materiality of the body is acknowledged and in the very same gesture redeemed by the Christian symbol of eternal life. The priest uses ash to make the sign of the cross on the believer's forehead, with the words, "Remember, man, that thou art dust, and unto dust thou shall return." If *The Waste Land* defines the terrain of the abject, by its constant reminders of the corruptibility of the flesh and images of death, corpses, bodily fluids, waste, and rubbish, *Ash-Wednesday* defeats the power of horror, not by separating the spirit from the body, but by offering true redemption, namely the divine spirit incarnated in human form. Eliot was no transcendentalist mystic. He was certainly a Christian believer but he understood, as did his Roman Catholic contemporaries Graham Greene and Evelyn Waugh, the necessity of recognizing the human state in all its fallen and tragic forms as still penetrated, in those very forms, by divine grace. Even if the subject does not recognize the divine presence, it is there doing its work. This is the poem's principal theme, not the process of Christian conversion as proposed by so much of the critical commentary on the poem.

Ash-Wednesday offers a personal narrative of recognition, acknowledgment, and change by a speaker who has already affirmed a faith but who needs to understand the human or existential dimensions of belief. That is why *Ash-Wednesday* begins with the halting, stammering voice of an abject humanity:

> Because I do not hope to turn again
> Because I do not hope
> Because I do not hope to turn   (*CP* 95)

The motif of "turning" is crucial in completing the process of recognition and acknowledgment. The poem defines the process of construing a renewed subjectivity, now more fully aware of its fateful encounter with the divine spirit. The abject is not erased by this widening of consciousness; it is simply put in its proper place. Part II of the poem begins with an evocation of the body devoured by animals, "three white leopards," who have "fed to satiety" on the speaker's legs, heart, liver, and brain. They have left "bones," "guts," the "strings of my eyes," and the "indigestible portions" of the body (97). In the waste land these human remains possessed the power to subvert meaning and order. They left the subject in disarray, fragmented, and deeply anxious. In *Ash-Wednesday* their power to disturb is not entirely diminished, but now there is a counter-movement and its proper form is prayer:

> Lady of Silences
> Calm and distressed
> Torn and most whole
> Rose of memory
> Rose of forgetfulness . . .   (97–98).

The whole prayer in Part II introduces paradox as the rhetorical form of the reborn subject, in recognition of the possibility of two truths existing as one. The Rose in the garden symbolizes this state rather well. It is, of course, a traditional symbol, but it helps to think of a real rose as well as the Rose of literary convention. The Rose of literature often symbolizes the perfection of an ideal love. It is also a sign of the spirit and its place as the culminating symbol at the conclusion of Dante's *Paradiso* gives it a divine character. Yet the real rose, the flower in a garden, is on reflection a peculiar choice to symbolize spiritual values. The real rose is seriously sensuous: its dramatic fragrances have the power to intoxicate, its petals are velvety to the touch, and their dense, erotic clustering make the head heavy in weight. Perhaps purely spiritual values are not precisely what the Rose as symbol is meant to convey. Rather than the ideal, the rose offers the perfect symbol of the incarnate state, materiality and spirituality in a single image. The corruptibility of matter and the incorruptible idea knotted in a single object makes the rose/Rose an apt metaphor for the subjectivity that the poem is laboring to discover.

This new subject has a number of aspects but none is more important than his reconsideration of what it means to be an artist, a poet in fact who has mastered his *métier*. In the new context of faith, the facility that comes with mastery of an art suddenly becomes suspect. If you are committed to living in truth, you must learn that self-satisfaction in accomplishment and polish mislead us; they put us on a false path to the various sins of narcissistic self-regard masquerading as artistic destiny. A Christian poet, however, must learn the way over rougher ground and that means being able to see through his own facile posturings. Even in the early poetry, Eliot played with the idea of control, another lesson learned from Laforgue. He began to subvert the traditional sense of poetic poise and purpose by amusing himself with the dialectic of mastery and incompetence. In the early monologues it appears as the framework of the persona's submission to paralysis. Prufrock imagines a sovereign self, but is too ham-fisted to carry it off. In "Portrait of a Lady" the speaker's "self-possession gutters . . . in the dark" (*CP* 21). In "Hysteria" the horrified male hopes to concentrate his "attention with careful subtlety" on the task of stopping "the shaking . . . breasts" (*CP* 34) of his female companion at tea.

The loss of mastery is most pronounced in the fragmentary texture of the final lines of *The Waste Land*. There the speaker succumbs to what has threatened the poem all along, the subject's miserable surrender to abjection. The "Notes" to the poem also silently address the matter of competence. But this time readers are the target; their sheer presence ridicules those whose incompetence in recognizing their own cultural inheritance is called mockingly into question. The stammering with which Part I opens daringly puts the whole matter of mastery in the lap of the poet. Eliot brings the issue to its final and most important stage, the master poet's public display of renunciation of his mastery. The public self-exposure marks the end of an early poetic persona and points us toward the birth of the Christian poet. It will feature in *Four Quartets* in a number of passages but most seriously in the second part of the second canto of "Little Gidding."

Part III of *Ash-Wednesday* dramatizes the relinquishing of mastery in the figure of the spiral staircase and the ascent of the subject toward a new life. Although the ascent is spiritual, the struggle on the staircase is primarily moral. As the subject ascends he looks back at a former self struggling with "the devil of the stairs who wears / The deceitful face of hope and despair" (*CP* 99). Leaving that "shape twisted" behind him, he passes higher through self-loathing and the enchantments of art. Here we find some of the most lyrical imagery in the poem, "a slotted window bellied like the fig's fruit" or "Blown hair is sweet, brown hair over the mouth blown, / Lilac and brown hair." As beguiling as these images are, they are, in a word, "Distraction," and as the subject climbs the third stair, they fade, to be replaced by the pilgrim's cry, "Lord, I am not worthy." The enchanted "maytime," it seems, stands in the way of the "word" which the subject now wants to hear: "but speak the word only." In Part IV he acknowledges that the "fiddles and the flutes" (100) must be borne away. The new regime brings restoration and redemption from pain and despair. But it does not erase the pain. Indeed, in Part IV we are asked to be mindful ("Sovegna vos") of the hurt of one in Dante's *Purgatorio* (Canto XXVI), Arnaut Daniel, the Provençal troubadour. He addresses to Dante a short, mournful speech in his native Provencal:

Ara vos prec, per aquella valor
que vos guida al som de l'escalina
sovenha vos a temps de ma dolor.

(Now I pray you, by that power
which guides you to the summit of the stair.
in due time, be mindful of my pain.)

Be mindful of my pain! You might be able to gain the topmost rung of the ladder of divine bliss, but the victory will be incomplete, indeed no victory at all, if you forget human pain and suffering.

Part V backs away slightly from the personal engagement of the previous four parts to meditate on the status of the word of God, the Word in short, in a world where it is "unspoken, unheard" (102). That the Word is not visibly potent in a secularist world may be a shame, but it is not fatal to the Word itself. The presence of the Word is not harmed by the fact that most are deaf to it. The poem acknowledges both the presence of God, even in his seeming absence, and the Word as revelation of His presence. Even as "the unstilled world still whirled," at its center "the silent Word" abides. Both those who "chose" "the place of grace" and those who "oppose" it can have the benefit of its offered power. Prayer is the form of the communion with grace and the poem asks "the veiled sister" to pray for all without doctrinal distinctions. She is asked to pray even "for those who offend her / And are terrified and cannot surrender" (103). The repeated phrase, "O my people," reaffirms the catholicity of grace's potency. The Word, it seems, is another face of the Incarnation. It is *in* the world but not *of* the world. The word of God is man's, yet man lives exiled from it. The Word is everywhere, yet the world seems opposed to it.

The final part of the poem returns us to the theme of transformation and to the voice of the uncertain supplicant. But instead of the causal relationship suggested by "Because I do not hope to turn again," the restatement makes a subtle shift in responsibility. "Although I do not hope to turn again" (104) moves from causality to concession. The subject is now better placed to accept the work of grace. He is able to see from "the wide window" something of the beauty of the world and a new lyricism comes into the text, "white sails . . . seaward flying," "Unbroken wings" instead of "merely vans to beat the air" (96) in Part I. The note of hope modulates into a quickening recovery from the despair with which the poem began. The prayer to the "Blessèd sister, holy mother" (105) asks for help in avoiding the self-mockery of falsehood and suffering of separation. The vision at the end is not transcendental; it cannot be defined as the desire to escape from the world into the pure bliss of the spirit. It was the Incarnation now put forward as the real meaning of faith. We cannot escape our human fate, but we are vouch-safed glimpses of holiness in the midst of the encompassing tragedy. This is not a special trick of the eye, it is what we see as an integral part of the reality we all share, if . . ., if we care to look. And the concrete reality that Eliot faced in the 1930s was not an ideal abstraction invented to house the new spiritual order. It was England and his life there in which the hidden order of grace moved.

Plays

After the publication of *Ash-Wednesday*, Eliot entered a short fallow period as far as his poetry was concerned. His creative work shifted significantly from poetry to drama and to cultural criticism. He had been interested in the theatre from his first introduction to the Elizabethan dramatists, but he had only explored their work critically. After 1933, he begins to think in terms of a practitioner. He had tried his hand at verse drama with *Sweeney Agonistes* in the 1920s but had got tangled up in generic and thematic issues that he could not resolve. This was principally because he had no sturdy story to tell, only an assemblage of music hall turns, allegorical figures, and jazz syncopations that led nowhere. Later, when he came to write *Murder in the Cathedral* (1935), he would have what was lacking in *Sweeney Agonistes*, a strong character, a strong narrative, and an important personal theme. The play dramatizes the murder of Thomas à Becket in Canterbury Cathedral in the twelfth century, exploring the theme of martyrdom and the logic of submission to God's will. The play dovetailed neatly with his work in support of the Church of England and made him one of the pillars of Anglicanism at a time when the Church and religion in general had entered their long decline. Eliot fought passionately against this trend and published an important statement about the centrality of religion to society in 1939 in *The Idea of a Christian Society*. His work on the religious pageant play *The Rock* (only the choruses have been preserved) in 1934 had earned him much gratitude from Church authorities, though it gained him little credit in literary circles. *Murder in the Cathedral* was a different matter. It was recognized as not only an important work on a religious theme but as an interesting contribution to theatre in terms of technique and structure. The play struck a chord in its time and his use of what for all intents and purposes is a Brechtian ending, when Becket's murderers step forward and address the audience, suggests Eliot's continued openness to experiment and innovation.

The success of *Murder in the Cathedral* whetted Eliot's appetite for the theatre and he threw himself into writing a new play, *The Family Reunion*, which was staged in 1939. The war interrupted the flow of theatrical work for about six years, but he quickly returned to drama afterward, composing three plays in eleven years: *The Cocktail Party* in 1948 (perhaps his most successful play), *The Confidential Clerk* in 1954, and *The Elder Statesman* in 1959. All these works dramatized the lives of middle-class individuals searching for significance in a secular world.

His plays, all written in blank verse, helped to create a taste for verse drama from the mid-1930s to the late 1950s. It was not a style of dramatic writing that would last but, for a time, it had its champions – Eliot himself, W. H. Auden in his collaborations with Christopher Isherwood, Ronald Duncan, Anne Ridler, Montagu Slater, and, above all, Christopher Fry. Eliot had helped to reinvent for the twentieth century a dramatic practice of the late sixteenth and early seventeenth centuries. He had taken a tradition of verse drama, which he had approached critically in the 1920s, and brought it to life on the contemporary stage.

Cultural criticism

After *Ash-Wednesday*, Eliot's energies were also taken up with the crisis which Europe entered in the 1930s. This occasioned a number of works of cultural criticism that addressed the social and political history of his time. As mentioned in Chapter 1, in 1932 he traveled to America to lecture at his alma mater, Harvard University. He had decided to give lectures drawn from materials he had been working with for the past fifteen years, which essayed a reevaluation of the tradition of English poetry and criticism. The lectures were published in late 1933 as *The Use of Poetry and the Use of Criticism*. On its publication this work helped to reshape, along the lines of Eliot's earlier critical thinking, the canon of English literature. Once highly authoritative, this critical work has for all intents and purposes lost its seminal force and is now simply an interesting episode in the evolution of English studies in England and America.

Eliot's other series of lectures in America has attracted more and more attention in recent years. At the University of Virginia in Charlottesville, he delivered the Page-Barbour lectures to an audience of southern gentlemen academics. It was a comfortable setting for Eliot. As a Missourian he had first-hand knowledge of the kind of psychology and culture that his audience in Virginia possessed. In other words, he knew these people well and he was at ease in their company. For one thing, they were comfortably traditional in culture, politics, and – dangerously for Eliot – on all matters of race and race-mixing. As a result, Eliot seems to have let his guard down for he spoke with uncharacteristic viciousness, another sign of the abject man exacting a kind of shifty revenge on his phantom oppressors. With a suaveness that belies the brutality of his words, he attacked friend and foe alike. He shifted the ground of his critical standards from the carefully construed boundaries of the formalist critic, of seeing art as art and not another thing, to delimiting a wider locus of attention. In Charlottesville the health of the culture and society, not just of literature, is invoked at length for the first time. This concern had always been there in Eliot's work, but not so flagrantly deployed. Now he speaks of the dangers of "heresy" as a new phase of the clapped-out "romanticism" that had ruined the culture of the nineteenth century; the "orthodox" work becomes synonymous with the "classic" as the cornerstone of a healthy society. He sees certain political and demographic realities of modern times in a new light in the Old South. He is contemptuous of a "Liberalism" that has rotted the heart of American civilization. The immigrant population – he calls them legions of "foreign" invaders – has "adulterated . . . homogenous" (*ASG* 22) communities of kinship and longevity, a distinct people living for a long period of time in the same place.

In this unguarded moment, and no doubt abetted by the warm acclaim of his delighted listeners, Eliot goes over the mark. The Jews, he tells the assembly of white, male southerners, are undesirable in large numbers. He is especially condescending to reformed or secular Jewry, referring to the presence of "free-thinking Jews" (26) as particularly objectionable. All this might have remained private remarks to an appreciative audience bound together by fear of the changes transforming the modern world. But it was not to be. The contract with the Page-Barbour foundation stipulated that the lectures must find their way into print. *After Strange Gods: A Primer of Modern Heresy* appeared in 1934 and Eliot's intemperate remarks found their way into the public domain. They were to dog him for the rest of his life and beyond the grave.

The book appeared only once and was never reprinted. When it was published in the mid-1930s, it did not create a major stir. Eliot's objectionable observations about immigrants, Jews, and others merged quietly into the general prejudices of white Anglo-American society. A few voices objected to his characterizations, but they were muffled and soon forgotten. Some Jews, however, like the philosopher George Boas, who had been on friendly terms with Eliot, were deeply offended, and broke off contact with him immediately. The coarseness of Eliot's thought is perhaps what surprised his literary readers, except of course the out-and-out racists who would have assented most heartily to the sentiments about race had they come across the book. But the book was largely forgotten as it went out of print and out of mind. It was not until after the Second World War that it resurfaced in the light of the Holocaust. Of course, Eliot could not have known in Charlottesville in 1933 what was in store for European Jewry in the 1940s and it must be said that when the full scope of the horror in Central Europe was revealed he was stunned. Yet he never explicitly apologized for *After Strange Gods*. He went on to repeat and expand his cultural sociology in the 1948 *Notes Towards the Definition of Culture*, but his approach in this recasting of a conservative social vision was far more temperate in tone and idea than the earlier work.

As the crisis of the 1930s deepened and with the approach of war, Eliot's concern about the social and political catastrophe to come took on a new coloring. By 1938, when gas masks began to be distributed to the population in England, it was very clear that the twenty year period of peace was coming to an end. The rise of Adolf Hitler in Germany had reenergized the German state and after the Munich Crisis in November 1938 war seemed inevitable. His thinking about these matters was focused on two important activities, the book he published in 1939, *The Idea of a Christian Society*, and his participation in the discussions of a group of Christian intellectuals in Britain called the Moot. *The Idea of a Christian Society* began as a series of lectures examining the place of the Church in society. For Eliot, the Church lay at the heart of a civilized society. Without it society would fail, and he was able to point to the seeming inability of Western liberal democracy, with its addiction to materialism and the denial of the godly, to deal with the challenges of communism and fascism. Allegiance to the historical confessions of Europe was absolutely necessary and society should be organized around the institutions of faith rather than the institutions of secular power. All through the late 1930s he had argued for the preservation of Christian society in his commentaries in the *Criterion*. He warned, he argued, and he protested, but he could not be dismissed as a simple Jeremiah for he had worked on various committees convened by the Archbishop of Canterbury and the World Council of Churches in pursuit of his ideals.

He was also something of an activist in the tradition of the New England Eliots for whom institutions were the levers for changing the world. Like the conservative political philosopher Leo Strauss, Eliot believed that it was small groups of committed thinkers, exerting influence on decision-makers behind the scenes, who would have the greatest chance of creating stable and just societies. But more importantly, they would be able to persuade the powerful that it was their duty to preserve Christian values. It was to this end that Eliot participated in the meetings of a group of intellectuals convened by J. H. Oldham in 1937–38 who gathered two or three times year until July 1945. He attended regularly from 1938 to 1943. The discussions within the Moot helped Eliot to bring many of his ideas about society into clearer focus. *The Idea of a Christian Society* and *Notes Towards the Definition of Culture* were the direct result of his contact in the Moot with some of the best minds of his time: Karl Mannheim, Christopher Dawson, Reinhold Niebuhr, Walter Oakeshott, Michael Polanyi, Middleton Murry, Alec Vidler, and Philip Mairet, to name only a few.

The outbreak of a second great war in a generation, in September 1939, overtook the Moot but it did not stop it. Rather, the break in normal life, which the war brought, energized the circle and made its work more urgent than ever. Its aim was twofold: to determine what kind of society should emerge from the destruction of war, and how those Western traditions that embodied the core values of Western civilization could best be preserved. For Eliot, these issues were not exclusively political or social in nature; they were also deeply personal, involving his own spiritual development and his sense of self.

Four Quartets

As he carried on with his day job at Faber and Faber, and contributed to the discussions of the Moot, Eliot began to conceive of a new work of poetry. His new interest in drama was thrown off course by the need, under conditions of total war, to close many public places, including theaters and as a result, his creative energies returned to his first love, poetry. He realized that "Burnt Norton," the poem he had composed in 1935, could be extended into a suite of poems centered on various geographical locations that would act as compass points of a whole life.

"Burnt Norton" defined a moment of visionary innocence both in and out of time. "East Coker," his family's English place of origin, provided the second sacred site in this personal pilgrimage through, but ultimately beyond, self-knowledge to a wider spiritual insight. "East Coker" was written in 1940. "The Dry Salvages," written in 1941, remembered his American origins both in Missouri and in New England. The final poem, "Little Gidding," composed in 1942, located the pilgrim's destination in an English religious context. The small chapel at Little Gidding took Eliot back to the Tudor and Stuart periods in English history, defining, for him, the essence of English civilization in an ambiguous historical moment, the defeat of

Charles I in the Civil War of the 1640s and the continuity of spiritual life as embodied in the small but devout Anglican community of Nicholas Ferrar at Little Gidding. The visionary experience at the end of the poem recalls, but goes beyond, the visionary moment in the garden in "Burnt Norton."

When the four poems were finished, Eliot collected them under one title, *Four Quartets*, and published them as a single work in 1944. The suite represents Eliot's highest achievement as a poet. *The Waste Land* is certainly a unique performance in the canon of twentieth-century poetry, but *Four Quartets* surpasses the earlier masterpiece. It is a supremely complete work that spoke eloquently and honestly to a destitute time. It was a very personal poem, even confessional in nature, that resonated with a new generation of readers confronting not only a psychological and emotional crisis, as in the 1920s, but an era of physical and moral destruction unparalleled in human history. There is nothing maudlin about it. Eliot's maturity as a man and as an artist is visible everywhere in the four parts. *Four Quartets* marks Eliot's turn in mid-century to a neoclassicism that is also visible in the work of other writters, the poet W. H. Auden for instance, and in the work of a composer like Igor Stravinsky. Eliot's prose essays of the time, "What is a Classic?" and "Johnson as Critic and Poet," both written in 1944, make his commitments to classicism explicit.

Yes, *Four Quartets* was personal, but it was also the most public of poems. It approached the ordinary reader without any of the murkiness of *The Waste Land*. It was not an easy poem, but it did not confound its readers with esoteric learning and an unseizable form. With unaffected dignity, and by striking the right balance between intimacy and elevation, Eliot found a way to perform the public duty of offering succor to frightened people in a dark time. This was a duty that only poetry could perform. One could apply to Eliot himself what he wrote about the wisdom and poetry of Goethe: "The wisdom is an essential element in making the poetry; and it is necessary to apprehend it as poetry in order to profit by it as wisdom" ("Goethe as the Sage," *PP* 223). The poem addressed its first readers as poetry and it is as poetry that it remains one of the great literary texts of the last century. What it had to offer as wisdom spoke to an England in crisis and, unlike *The Waste Land*, a poem that began as a very personal poem but incidentally ended up defining an era, *Four Quartets* was intentionally public even as it explored themes and places that were highly personal.

With the passing of the historical context in which it was written, the poem has lost something of its public importance. It has become in time a very private poem about matters of the spirit. But it is more than that. Indeed, let me say, without fear of contradiction, that *Four Quartets* was the last poem in

English that was written for and read by the wider reading public. It was perhaps the last time in the English-speaking world that serious poetry was read as both personally relevant and as a guide to the fate of one's time. You can see the marks of this attention to the readership beyond literary coteries in the general character of its language and form. Certain formal considerations – the five-part development, the alternation of familiar lyric modes, the musical recurrence of image and phrase motifs, the classical refinement of the speaking voice – give the sequence a discernible homogeneity, as opposed to *The Waste Land* with its collage-like interplay of lyric voices, prophetic incantation, and popular speech. The voice of *Four Quartets*, on the other hand, finds its specific gravity in a kind of classic poise. We know rather well what a phrase like "classic poise" might mean because in the same year as the publication of the whole *Four Quartets*, Eliot addressed the Virgil Society on the theme of "What is a Classic?"

In this essay Eliot defines what one might mean by calling a work of art "classic." He mentions three features linked by a common thread. Maturity of mind, maturity of manners, and maturity of language are the three principal attributes of the classic work. These maturities require a corresponding maturity in the audience, in the "age" as Eliot puts it. Of course, this definition begs the question of what constitutes maturity, but that is a word that most will know from their own experience rather than as a term in a professional critical vocabulary. We may not know what "classic" means, but we all know maturity when we see it. In communicating to his "age," the master must also contract a style, a "common style," that brings to maximum fulfillment all the language's resources in the task of communicative comprehensiveness and universality. It cannot aim too high and it cannot go too low in terms of diction and linguistic register. Indeed, it requires the achievement of a kind of purity that is foreign to the cultural politics of the early twentieth-century avant-garde in which Eliot cut his teeth. The word purity recalls a passage by the French poet Stéphane Mallarmé that Eliot uses in "Little Gidding":

> Since our concern was speech and speech impelled us
> To purify the dialect of the tribe . . .
>
> ("Little Gidding," *CP* ll. 126–127).

Mallarmé's sense of the purity of language stems from an aesthetic concern, that is to say, that a true work of art posits an idiom all its own, divorced from the social impurities of the languages of everyday life. The language of poetry aspires to a condition that Mallarmé calls *poésie pur*. Early in his life as a poet, Eliot was drawn to this kind of symbolist approach, but by the 1940s his point of view had shifted. Purity may be a concern as an aspect of modernist aesthetics, but it was also now a concern in a purely social sense. In a time of war and crisis, it was necessary to make poetry speak a common tongue. In fact, when he used the word "purity" in his 1932–33 lectures at Harvard, published as *The Use of Poetry and the Use of Criticism*, Eliot had already begun to move away from the symbolist practices of the French poets that he so admired as a young man. He does not talk about the making of a pure art-language as the highest expression of poetic intent. In a passage on difficult poetry, he talks about a "seasoned reader" who "has reached . . . a state of greater *purity*" (*Use* 151, italics in original) in understanding that a poem may do its work even though the formal meaning may not be imme-diately available. Increasingly, Eliot developed a more acute sense of the reader's presence in the act of composition and the need for the poet to connect with the community at large. His interest in drama and his many years of experience as an editor attuned him to the mindset of particular readers and their habits. Any other approach seemed merely self-indulgent and irresponsible.

The readers of *Four Quartets* were not simply taking in poetry for its own sake. In the midst of the war crisis, works of art took on a greater importance. Apart from their intrinsic qualities, they were judged in terms of morale, whether they helped people face up to their situation or undermined their resolve. *Four Quartets* ministered to morale, though there were some, such as George Orwell, who found in them something like a defeatist attitude. Generally, though, the poems were read in a positive light. Of course, we should not mistake them for propaganda. They worked more deeply and intelligently than simple partisanship. There were a number of ways in which they communicated their seriousness. One was the musical form which the overall title invoked. The quartet is an intimate but strict genre built on sonata principles that provided Eliot with just the right combination of structure and flexibility. The free play of familiar and intelligent instrumental "voices," within a limited formal space, gave Eliot a chance to use his talent for voices but to restrict them to a small number. In a musical quartet the four instruments carry on an intimate conversation allowing for the devel-opment of theme and subject. *Four Quartets* also alternates a series of voices conversationally – Keith Alldritt in *Poetry as Chamber Music* (1978) believes there are four of them – in order to develop recurring themes.[21] The choice of the quartet gave Eliot a form that was intimate, in that the four instruments carry on an intimate conversation, but in a publicly accessible way. In this way, the poet speaks privately to each of us, but none of us is excluded from his address. This is key to the poem's affect, its design on the reader.

The intimacy of chamber music suggests an openness and an honesty of address that provide Eliot with another way of establishing the poem's gravity. The principal rhetorical strategy of *Four Quartets* is to maintain that it is not rhetorical. This is achieved in a number of ways. One way is through a reader's recognition of the kind of social voices which we hear in the text. The philosopher, the lyric poet, the confessional voice, the visionary, the conversationalist, and so on, are several possible verbal roles performed by the text. Dramatic monologue has been left far behind in this new procedure. These are all Eliot's voices and they address each of us as reader with a candor and confidence that is highly impressive. Indeed, the poem urges us from the first philosophical speculations about time in "Burnt Norton" to feel, to *feel*, not necessarily to understand rationally, that we are in the presence of an unflappable maturity. In this way, the poem constructs, silently, the ideal reader of the classic work of literature. At no point in the whole sequence does this sense of being in the presence of an unassailable maturity ever slacken. Even when the poet seems to indulge an adolescent taste for cosmic epic at the beginning of the second canto of "East Coker," in the passage beginning "What is the late November doing . . .", the mature voice quickly reasserts itself with a weary debunking of the exertion, "That was a way of putting it – not very satisfactory" ("East Coker," *CP* ll. 51–67, 68).

Maturity also implies that the poem does not simply offer a point of view or a perspective on matters of art, history, and religion, least of all a self-indulgent excursion in lyrical autobiography. It seems to work out past mere argument and position-taking. The real is its goal, not a way of looking at the real, but the real as such. That is why "Burnt Norton" begins with two epigraphs from the pre-Socratic philosopher Heraclitus and in the voice of the professional philosopher. The philosophical voice is not peddling mere rhetoric or sententiousness. It is infused with reason and not "merely chattering" ("Burnt Norton," *CP* l. 154). The philosopher's measured tone reminds us of a human inheritance that goes back 2,500 years to Heraclitus. That voice may also remind us of our own introduction to that legacy in our first schoolroom.

The affect is completed by Eliot's construction of a paradoxical scene of reading in the opening of "Burnt Norton." The words seem to be turned inward as the voice works its way toward a careful delineation of the truth; we are put in the position of overhearing the philosopher at work. The measured, familiar tone of voice does not really sound as if it is trying to convince us of anything. We hear the philosopher with his careful probing speech moving in the style of truth in the Western philosophical tradition. If we need comforting, we may very well remember this voice from the lecture theater and seminar room. Whatever feelings of disquiet and trepidation we may have in a time of crisis and approaching war, or even war itself, the composure of the voice calms us. We have no reason to fret about "What might have been" nor to regret "what has been." Instead, we must learn to live with what is and "is always present' (ll. 1–10). This finely crafted reserve is achieved with the simplest of means in the language of the poem, but it begins before the poem opens with the epigraphs from Heraclitus.

The first epigraph questions the validity of individual perspective. The translation of the whole fragment is as follows. Eliot cites only the second part: "Therefore one must follow (the universal Law, namely) that which is common (to all). But although the Law is universal, the majority live as if they had understanding peculiar to themselves."[22] We learn from this that an individual subject cannot gain knowledge of the *logos* on the basis of being a unique and separate individual. The epigraph declares that most men act as if they have insight of their own, rather than resigning themselves to their inherent partialness, and, thus, recognizing and accepting the universality of the *logos*, that which is common to all. The second epigraph – "The way up and down is one and the same"[23] – adds a new element to the first. It recovers for the present time a kind of reasoning from the dawn of thought itself. The language of paradox points us to ways of authoritative thinking that have been marginalized or displaced in an age of science and positivism. Paradox is the figure of thought that makes it possible to see, for example, that the Incarnation is not simply a mystical apparition, but a reality that has the power to redeem us.

The epigraphs and the philosophical voice give way after the first ten lines to a new register: "Footfalls echo in the memory." From line eleven to the end of the first canto of "Burnt Norton," the drama of primordiality is now pushed back further in a new way, no longer as knowledge or philosophy, but as personal experience. The events in "our first world" (l. 22) are recollected with imagist vividness that make lyric intensity not simply an aesthetic affect, but a complementary way of embracing the real. The pre-Socratic relationship between philosophy and poetry returns in a tone of quiet triumph. Eliot's evocation of the garden connects the personal experience of childhood and the first world of the Christians, the Garden of Eden. Of course, we know now that the experience was shaped also by a visit to the manor house at Burnt Norton in Gloucestershire in 1934. We are invited to follow the voice of the thrush into that first world of experience and to give ourselves to primal memories. The collapse of strict temporal distinctions leads to an extraordinary dilation of consciousness beyond the confining grammars of time. But why one might do this is left unresolved. It is almost as if we cannot help ourselves in the present moment of this calling. We must follow because, though the meaning is uncertain, the experience is not to be missed. As the passage moves toward its visionary climax, the vision glittering "out of heart of light" (l. 37) is not a mystical escape from reality but reality itself. But there is nothing comforting about this human approach to the real: "human kind / Cannot bear very much reality" (ll. 42–43) is the brutal truth that brings us back to earth and the consoling voice of the philosopher, if not exactly the consolations of philosophy which we now see as somewhat incomplete without poetry.

In the second canto the symbolist poet returns with a vengeance. References to Mallarmé's "Le Tombeau de Charles Baudelaire" and "M'introduire dans ton histoire" in the lyric which begins "Garlic and sapphires in the mud" recall earlier aesthetic commitments that have now been abandoned. The symbolist Eliot can still make great poetry in this manner, but we are aware that now it will not do. Later in "Burnt Norton," after another apocalyptic lyric of visionary power, Eliot will acknowledge the limitations of the symbolist aesthetic, indeed the limitations of poetry itself in the pursuit of something more valuable, namely, the separation of "inner freedom from the practical desire, / The release from action and suffering," the release from compulsion (ll. 70–71). The second part of this canto develops a number of paradoxical propositions; indeed, taking Heraclitus as guide, the poem makes paradox its central heuristic device. The dialectic of "still point" and "turning world" can only be developed by the series of paradoxes that follow. Such a procedure defeats the materialist reasoning of a scientific age, but it does reorient thinking so that the clinching line at the end of the canto – "Only through time time is conquered" (l. 90) – can make sense. This has a capital significance for Eliot, though it may mystify the uninitiated reader. It asserts the importance of an inward transformation that has the defeat of desire and attachment to the things of the world as its primary goal.

The third canto opens with what amounts to a traditional, medieval, contempt of "this twittering world" (l. 113) by the ascetic consciousness. We have reached "a place of disaffection" and the passage enumerates its difficulties. The lines are recognizably dismissive of a world of distraction, "empty of meaning" (l. 102), of pervasive gloom, and darkness. But this is not where Eliot stops. The poet does not simply reject the weary routines of everyday life and the traditional forms of salvation from the "Tumid apathy" (l. 103), but rejects experience itself. We are being asked to understand that we must "Descend lower" (l. 114) toward something the poem calls the "Internal darkness" (l. 117). This corresponds to a more radical stillness than can be imagined in a world bound to longing and desire or "appetency" moving "on its metalled ways" (l. 125). The ominous tone which enters the voice as we traverse the silence between the two halves of the third canto takes us past the familiar critique of the world's shallowness or ephemerality, into the metaphysical darkness of "that which is not world" (l. 116). The references to Dante's voyage into the inferno and the tradition of the *via negativa* in European mysticism, especially in the work of St. John of the Cross, are important points of reference and of construction for this part of Eliot's journey. Eliot's programme of renunciation is here made clear enough, no matter how completely moments of "lucid stillness" (l. 93) or the seeming "permanence" of "beauty" (ll. 94–95) might hide from us the world's undeniable transience.

This last point is emphasized in the fourth canto. The enchanting moments of vision, of "sunflower" (l. 129) and "kingfisher's wing" (l. 134), cannot hide from us that "Time and the bell" will bury the day (l. 127). These moments of lyric intensity may seem permanent and real, but they are not. They may carry us to the threshold of the eternal, but they cannot take us there. As one might expect, the whole poem insists repeatedly that time is an illusion. The parallel cantos in the remaining poems will elaborate this idea three more times with more concrete detail and with increasing resolve. But in these passages Eliot says something else as well. Renunciation occurs in the silence of interiority, as an inward action. This means abandoning ideas of significant action in the world, letting go the illusion that any involvement in the world matters in the scale of ultimate things. The subtle metaphysical speculations in the closing lines of the fifth canto lucidly expand on the theme of divine "Love" as "itself unmoving . . . Caught in the form of limitation / Between un-being and being" (ll. 163–168). It is this invocation of divine love that Eliot will build on in the rest of the sequence.

Divine love and divine grace cannot be made visible. Language can suggest their presence in the same way that we cannot see gravity but are free to walk on the earth without fear of falling headlong into space. But language cannot bring them fully to view. Woven through the sequence is the theme of the inadequacy of language in the pursuit of what is hidden from view, hidden from our day-to-day experience. This is perhaps why in "Burnt Norton" the descent reaches the place where experience itself is annulled as the road to redemption. The theme of language has been a central aspect of Eliot's poetry from the start and in *Four Quartets* the theme culminates as part of the inner meaning and greatness of the poem's form:

> Words strain,
> Crack and sometimes break, under the burden,

Under the tension, slip, slide, perish,
Decay with imprecision, will not stay in place.
Will not stay still.   (ll. 149–153)

The problem is put in the form of a double assault on the poet. One is external – words are assailed by demonic voices; the other is internal – the poet's human self, his ego perhaps, cannot avoid undermining the wider responsibility that the Christian poet would like to satisfy. The deeper significance of the passage as a whole is clear enough: words fail through their own inner limitations – they "Will not stay still" – and neither can the poet sit still even as he beseeches God to teach him how. Words, as well as egos, are in a perpetual state of insurgency; both "slip, slide, perish," and they do so "under the burden." "[T]he intolerable wrestle / With words and meanings" ("East Coker," ll. 71–72) is not merely an echo of the Flaubertian sense of the labor involved in finding form or in searching for *le mot juste* in discourse landscapes rutted by clichés and banalities. It recalls the sweat of Adam tilling a cursed ground or Jacob wrestling with the angel. Or Yeats remembering the hard labor of composition in "Adam's Curse." The point about language's inadequacy may rely on a point of Pauline theology as found in Romans 1:20: "For the invisible things of [God] from the creation of the world are clearly seen, being understood by the things that are made, *even* his eternal power and Godhead." The things that are made, that is to say, the visible things, "understand" the invisible things of God. The Platonism that lies behind this verse is clear enough: behind the visible there lies the invisible universe which is the origin of all concrete things. Karl Barth, in his great commentary on Paul's Epistle to the Romans brings this out very well: "The clear, honest eyes of the poet in the book of Job and of . . . Solomon had long ago rediscovered, mirrored in the world of appearance, the archetypal, unobservable, undiscoverable Majesty of God. The speech of God can always be heard out of the whirlwind."[24]

Is it possible to hear the speech or voice of God in a poem? The answer in *Four Quartets* seems to be no. The poem seems to direct us elsewhere. Nature is a possibility, the sound of the birds in the garden, the thrush, the river in "The Dry Salvages," the winter solstice in "Little Gidding," all these point us toward some apprehension of what lies hidden from view. In the end, it is the dead toward whom we are asked to attend.

. . . what the dead had no speech for, when living,
They can tell you, being dead: the communication
Of the dead is tongued with fire beyond the language of the
    living.   ("Little Gidding," ll. 49–51)

The final ecstatic vision of the incarnate Rose at the end of the sequence includes the infolding of the same "tongues of flame" (l. 257).

Yet within those limits, the brief clearing of eyes and ears allows us to see the flashes of "winter lightning" showing us for a moment that "the impossible union / Of spheres of existence is actual" ("The Dry Salvages," ll. 216–217). But seeing in this higher sense in Eliot's poetry is always momentary or fleeting. One always returns forlorn after this seeing to the everyday. One might compare this return to the trajectory of Keats's flight into sublimity and the descent therefrom in "Ode to a Nightingale." But I think we would be wrong. Being transported to a more replete reality by art is one thing, but for a Christian poet it is a form of deception. We cannot be satisfied or completed by entry into the "artifice of Eternity" as in Yeats's "Sailing to Byzantium." Art may bring us to the edge but it cannot take us there:

> Words, after speech, reach
> Into the silence.   ("Burnt Norton," ll. 139–140)

Words, *after* speech? This sounds suspiciously like one of those zen conundrums, known as koans: what is the sound of one hand clapping? Speech, we are told, the concrete text, the very poem we are reading perhaps, cannot take us there where the divine *logos* reigns. This is rather a disappointing place to end. Yet it is not the end.

Seeing may be momentary or fleeting, but hearing is another matter. In *The Use of Poetry and the Use of Criticism*, at the end of a discussion of Matthew Arnold, Eliot suddenly breaks off and writes one of those wonderful passages of critical theory which introduce a resonant phrase into the language of criticism that we still puzzle over, even as we use it. Eliot in that lecture is saying that Arnold was "so conscious of what, for him, poetry was *for*, that he could not altogether see it for what it is" (*Use* 118). And what is it? Eliot tells us that Arnold was "not highly sensitive to the musical qualities of verse." And this lack in Arnold gives Eliot the occasion for a general point: "What I call the 'auditory imagination' is the feeling for syllable and rhythm, penetrating far below the conscious levels of thought and feeling, invigorating every word; sinking to the most primitive and forgotten, returning to the origin and bringing something back, seeking the beginning and the end" (118–119).

This somewhat enigmatic passage has a reverberating vagueness that Eliot does not usually allow into his prose. The auditory imagination appears, for Eliot, to go below consciousness, but also back through the life of the race, to "the most primitive." In a note to the final chapter of the same book, he refers, approvingly I believe, to a French article suggesting that "the pre-logical mentality persists in civilised man, but becomes available only to or through the poet" (148). One can speculate (and it is no more than speculation) that the "origin" referred to is prelapsarian, Edenic, and that the "end" – in the expression "the beginning and the end," whose importance we know from *Four Quartets* – may look to the end of time.

Certainly, the poet's sensibility goes below articulate language, to a pre-linguistic as well as a prelogical state, reaching downward and back to wordless rhythm. Eliot writes on almost the last page of *The Use of Poetry and the Use of Criticism* that "Poetry begins, I dare say, with a savage beating a drum in a jungle, and it retains that essential of percussion and rhythm; hyperbolically one might say that the poet is older than other human beings" (155). The auditory imagination defines a potentiality in all languages in all places for the ear to hear, through the rare moments of achieved poems, what Barth was referring to when he wrote, *à propos* Romans 1:20, that the "speech of God can always be heard out of the whirlwind".[25] This does not mean that we can understand it or even know from whom it comes. The great poem penetrates below the conscious articulations of mind, and of civilization, by displacing the deposits of noise, din, clatter, racket in our heads so that what is most ancient and, paradoxically, what is to come, the beginning and the end, can remake us.

Yet we are all still immersed in time and history, and when we turn to the three quartets written and published during the war, history, historical forms of knowing, and the relation of history to eternity come more clearly into focus. "Burnt Norton" has given us the metaphysical foundations; "East Coker" broaches more concretely the question of historical forms of time. Eliot's meditation on history weaves in and out of the remaining poems, concluding with the explicit propositions about history in the third canto of "Little Gidding" (ll. 150–199). The poems quietly but firmly oppose all those concepts of history that emphasize its chronological, empirical, progressive, and ameliorative character. Eliot's views contest the received positivist and materialist traditions of the eighteenth-century Enlightenment. He also opposed the nineteenth-century passion for historical forms of knowing, perhaps best illustrated by the shift in theology from the word of God as a transcendental idea outside of the merely temporal to the pursuit of the historical roots of Christianity and of the effort to discover the historical Jesus. His opposition to these ideas had several important consequences, but perhaps most telling for his present purpose was the need to displace narrative as the human discourse best organized to convey historical reality. When we are immersed in the ongoing story of the human prospect, we are not well positioned to notice the significance of a nonnarrative, nonchronological concept of history. But this is where Eliot asks us to look. For him, the importance of history and the moment in history only occurs when it intersects with eternity. The conventional view of history gives way to what we might call history as lyric repletion. History as sequential, the steady course of temporal activities, is occasionally disjointed by the sudden "shaft of sunlight" ("The Dry Salvages," *CP* l. 208) which for an instant – "Quick now, here, now, always" ("Little Gidding," l. 252) – registers the presence of the divine in and out of time.

This is the familiar distinction between history as *chronos* and history as *kairos*, between time as mere succession that just goes on and those intense moments of revelation in which time stops. When things or events are charged with a "seasonal" meaning, "a meaning [is] derived from its relation to the end."[26] For Eliot, "history is a pattern / Of timeless moments" ("Little Gidding," ll. 234–235), moments of personal vision, private meaning, and Christian revelation. *Four Quartets* works to lift consciousness free of perpetual entanglement in *chronos*. By lowering history to a level of diminished significance, it becomes easier to dismiss it. History is no longer seen as Necessity, the all-encompassing temporal prison we must all endure, but as a limited domain, from which we are occasionally freed by "the moment in and out of time" ("The Dry Salvages," l. 207).

After "Burnt Norton," the following three quartets each take up one aspect of historical time. "East Coker" addresses the theme of family history, biographically relevant to the origin of Eliot's own ancestors in Somerset, where the village is located. Dynastic time – "In succession / Houses rise and fall" ("East Coker," ll. 1–2) – the rhythm of the generations, the persistent return of the old as the new and back again, the sense of time as ceaseless reiteration, all imply the illusory character of typical liberal-humanist ideas of progress and the ideals of human improvement. We are returned to Eliot's seminal essay on tradition and the individual talent: art, or in this case history, never improves, but the materials are never the same. This crucial idea informs Eliot's later cultural criticism, principally *The Idea of a Christian Society* (1939) published just months before "East Coker" and the *Notes Towards the Definition of Culture*. History may be illusion, but this is no reason to ignore it or to believe that it is epistemologically negligible. Its status, however, is emblematic rather than empirical. It offers us images and symbols but leaves us free of particular narratives, concrete events, and necessary obligations. The evocation of the country festival, with which the first canto of "East Coker" concludes, works precisely as a symbol of a harmonious, integrated society located in Elizabethan England but here lifted out of time as an enduring archetype of an unchanging, hierarchical rural culture which persists continuously in a nation's collective consciousness even if it can no longer be found in the real world. The dancing countrymen "In that open field . . . Holding eche other by the hand or the arm / Whiche betokeneth concorde" (ll. 23–33) projected an irresistible vision of communal harmony and solidarity. In the conditions of wartime, especially through its darkest days, the emblem of unity coincided with the efforts to embolden the people of Britain in the face of war.

Having been reassured by such a vision of the English past, how could a reader then resist Eliot's more telling advice to adopt a disinterested attitude to history in the third cantos of "The Dry Salvages" and "Little Gidding"? In the former the use of the Hindu holy texts, the *Bhagavad Gita* and the *Upanishads*, as sources only underlined the idea of detachment. Eliot's thoughts in the third canto of "The Dry Salvages" are more subtle than a simple counsel of detachment from the world. The way of the recluse is not what he is recommending. His views are also Christian and, as a result, he is conscious of death as the destination of human life. But it is the making concrete of a paradoxical experience, "the moment which is not action or inaction" ("The Dry Salvages," l. 155), that brings together both Hindu and Christian traditions. The preparation for "the time of death," and he reminds us that this time "is every moment" (ll. 159–161), means that our involvement with things and with the world must have a particular character. We must "fare forward" (l. 168) but not entangled in its snares. We must be *in* the world but not *of* it. We are, in brief, exiles, but exiles with responsibilities and obligations that we cannot abandon. The actions, beliefs, and events which constitute our experience should not be seen as constituting a matrix of determinations which the subject can never escape. Neither should the future be seen as the horizon of further inescapable entanglements.

We can be sure that time will not heal us (ll. 130–131) and there is no redemption either through "action or inaction" in history. While we are in time we can only fare forward detachedly, having heard the voice of our calling, that is, of our being called to death:

> At nightfall, in the rigging and the aerial,
> Is a voice descanting (though not to the ear,
> The murmuring shell of time, and not in any language)   (ll. 146–148)

This is Eliot's restatement of what it means to be a Christian in the world: the subject, like Dante's famous boat in the second canto of *Paradiso* (l. 3), must make its way forward, but it must make its way singing. The musical "voice descanting" dismisses the notion of history as necessary narrative both in the individual life and in society. Our involvement in the world can be simultaneously affirmed and set aside for the inner detachment of the enchanted singing. In the third canto of "Little Gidding" Eliot returns to detachment as the form of our active engagement with life and history. The use of memory is important because it liberates us by expanding love beyond desire. At this point we must remember that desire is at the root of abjection. If we can abandon desire of things and people, we will find that history may be both "servitude" and "freedom" ("Little Gidding," ll. 162–163) and that it does not matter which it is. The strife that appears to divide us into parties and factions seems real enough and it can certainly make us abject, but love in this new sense takes us beyond faction. In a passage adapted from the English medieval mystic Julian of Norwich, Eliot brings this discussion to a close with the consoling words of the sage: sin is inevitable, she writes, but no matter what "All shall be well, and / All manner of thing shall be well" (ll. 167–168).

The meditation on history offers a way of engaging with life without losing oneself in the world. The poem works to persuade the doubtful reader by adopting a tone of conciliation and self-revelation. Indeed, it is possible to say that in *Four Quartets* Eliot even adopts a kind of confessional mode. The intent is inclusive, to bring all readers into the poet's confidence and to show his good faith by revealing something of himself. It is a risky undertaking because confession can seem self-indulgent and narcissistic and, as a result, negate the connection with the reader that the procedure is meant to create. Of course, all works of art are confessional in some sense, all acts of language reveal something of the author. But Eliot makes self-revelation and confession a thematic concern of *Four Quartets*. This is one of the roads he takes, paradoxical as it seems, to arrive at one of the poem's crucial Christian destinations, humility. The confessional mode is used as a way of opening new areas of feeling that originate in an exacting self-scrutiny. This voice takes us wherever self-examination may lead, no matter how arduous. An authentic humility cannot be earned any other way.

It is a very disarming thing to have a poet turn around after a magnificent performance in the apocalyptic visionary mode – the first part of the second canto in "East Coker" for example, "What is the late November doing . . ." (ll. 51–67) – and to write it off as "not very satisfactory" and "worn-out" (ll. 68–69). It certainly undermines the satisfactions which mastery of an art or knowledge is supposed to give us. In a sense, what it teaches is not necessarily humility, but that mastery can take many forms, including, paradoxically, its surrender. "The poetry does not matter" (l. 71) because individuals ought to be directed to other ends which poetry cannot fully comprehend. We are meant to read these lines about poetry and its limits in close conjunction with the lines about music in the fifth canto of "Burnt Norton." These points are reprised and expanded in the fifth canto of "East Coker." Confessional inflections provide, in the context of self-examination, a style for exploring interiority in a new way. We are taken into the poet's confidence, backstage as it were, where we hear the great artist gently mocking his own performance. The disarming candor and intimacy of "That was a way of putting it" or "So here I am, in the middle way" ("East Coker," l. 172) are repeated again in the second canto of "The Dry Salvages" – "It seems, as one becomes older, . . ." (l. 85) – and again, more compellingly still, in the parallel canto of "Little Gidding" – "In the uncertain hour before the morning . . ." (l. 78).

It is in this second part of the second canto of "Little Gidding" that we see the extraordinary final effect of the confessional mode in *Four Quartets*. Having been accustomed in each of the preceding quartets to expect a kind of conversational lowering of the temperature after the lyrical opening, Eliot's adaptation of Dante's *terza rima* is both surprising and inevitable. Lying, tonally, somewhere between the freer fluencies of "That was a way of putting it" and the prosodically compressed and rhymed lyric mode, this is impassioned, metrical speech, yet with all the rhythmical virtues of supple, heightened prose left intact. This style is chosen as the best way to convey, finally, naked confession, confession of the ghostly, composite "master" which we are now asked to overhear. The style encourages us to accept the passage as the wisdom of experience, not as contentious issues about which we can have opinions and views. These are truths through and through. The poem implies that they can be acquired only by the greatest self-discipline and detachment from self and the world. They constitute the clearest possible statement of what exactly this "reality" is of which humankind cannot bear very much in "Burnt Norton." The master offers to "disclose the gifts reserved for age," those which "set a crown upon your lifetime's effort" (ll. 129–130 and *passim*). Reality lies not in some exaggerated sense of great evil but closer to home, in awareness of our simple deceits, lusts, impotence, in short, all our ordinary wickednesses. It ends with "rending pain" (l. 138) and spiritual exasperation (l. 144).

The sense of a heroic stripping bare of all personal artifice is already present in embryo in the experience of "enchainment" to desire and "the weakness of the changing body" in "Burnt Norton" (ll. 79–80). It is given a bloated life as the epic simile *en double* of the theater and the underground train in the third canto of "East Coker" (ll. 113–121). And, again, the faces in the third canto of "The Dry Salvages" relaxing "from grief into relief" (l. 135) on yet another train journey. But it is in the final quartet that this line of development reaches its most consummate formulation. The approval of fools and the public honors heaped on a smiling public man exasperates the spirit ("Little Gidding," ll. 143–144). Only the most drastic measures of self-scrutiny, renunciation, and atonement can bring about the "at-one-ment" with truth that restores us. The closing reference to "that refining fire" which brings about the long-sought restoration, in concert with the fire imagery in all the *Four Quartets*, prepares the reader for the vision of rose and fire to come.

Reevaluation

Some critics and scholars of twentieth-century literature contend that with the passage of time Eliot's significance in the literary culture of his time needs to be reassessed. A reevaluation of his poetry and criticism needs to be undertaken in the same spirit in which he urged the reevaluation of literary history as he found it in the period of the First World War. Other poets from his generation have emerged, some critics say, as figures of greater consequence. His putative anti-Semitism and misogyny have turned some readers away from his work. Although these attitudes can be found in the academy, it is rather remarkable that Eliot remains for the wider reading public and in the culture more generally a recognizable figure. The use of his children's book about cats, *Old Possum's Book of Practical Cats* (1950), in one of the most popular musical shows in stage history has certainly kept him in the news.

This remarkable piece, which has given so much pleasure to millions of people either in book form or as the popular musical, did what none of Eliot's other works ever could. It reached the masses. His other works are widely read no doubt, but mainly by generally well-educated readers with an interest in culture. *Cats* speaks to everyone, whether they are great lovers of cats or not. Indeed, the volume brings out an aspect of the man's personality that is very rarely revealed. Delight, humor, evanescent verbal play are not words that leap to our minds when we think of Thomas Stearns Eliot, Poet. Yet they describe this complicated man as well as any other epithet. The poems were written for children. They were private productions for the enjoyment of a friend's family with whom Eliot would spend happy holidays in the 1930s. The children loved them, and of all Eliot's poems they are the ones the world has come to know the best. He would have noticed the irony of this situation and, one might speculate, would have found it delicious.

In terms of popular discourse, Eliot is probably the most-quoted poet of the twentieth century. Phrases from "The Love Song of J. Alfred Prufrock," *The Waste Land*, and *Four Quartets* have lodged in popular speech as names of other books, films, even songs, and as a variety of common sayings. And his poetry still bulks large in the curricula of schools and universities. His uncanny ability to capture the spirit of his time continues to bring readers to his work. The modern world he faced is still in many respects the very world with which we must deal. The personal crises that shaped his life – a bad marriage, the sense of lost traditions and community, the search for a spiritual solution in a secular world – still resonate with many people in the twenty-first century.

The importance of his poetry needs no emphasis, but perhaps, today, the radical nature of his literary criticism does. No one needs reminding that Eliot was the moving force behind the reorientation of Anglo-American literary criticism in the first half of the twentieth century. This involves more than simply doing better what others, in the nineteenth century, had already done. He was not in any serious sense, as some scholars have argued, Arnold's successor. His criticism represents as decisive a break with the past as "The Love Song of J. Alfred Prufrock" breaks with the line of English poetry. First of all, he insisted on dealing with a poem as a poem "and not another thing." That this reading *in vacuo* was said to produce finer accuracies of affect and intellect obscured a converse blindness that yielded other kinds of exactitude, the indeterminate pointedness of silence, often poetic, sometimes political. He also believed that it was only by comparative analysis of specific passages of a work that its meaning and significance could be ascertained. His sense that a literary field was defined not by absolute or ancient standards but by a self-governing system of changing values led him to revise the accepted ideas of tradition inherited from the Victorians. His methods of close reading harmonized very well with other, modernist modes of reading, "practical criticism" in England and "new criticism" in America. Emphasizing close verbal analysis, the comparative method, and the close reading of form, Eliot's new style of critical analysis helped to supplant both the philological methods of the nineteenth-century scholar and the *belles lettres* approach of the amateur critic and reviewer.

His efforts in disrupting old ideas of tradition meant that some of the most revered writers in the Victorian canon were relegated to a lesser role in the new literary history. John Milton, the Romantics, Alfred, Lord Tennyson, and Algernon Swinburne were taken down several notches and Dante, the other poets of the Italian *trecento*, Donne, the metaphysical poets in general, Andrewes, Baudelaire, and the French symbolists, especially minor figures such as Jules Laforgue and Tristan Corbière, were raised to new heights, much to the astonishment of the literary establishment. The share of criticism and theory today has been in large part fashioned by the ideas that Eliot helped to put in circulation in the 1920s. This may not be something that all scholars and critics would like to acknowledge, but there is no doubt that T. S. Eliot remains a central figure and will do so for a good long time to come.

Chapter 4

Critical reception

It was *The Waste Land* that launched Eliot as a public man. Overnight he was known to a readership wider than the small bohemian coterie in London with which he was associated after his arrival there in 1914. His 1917 volume, *The Love Song of J. Alfred Prufrock and Other Observations*, had gained the notice of the avant-garde poetry scene in London and to some extent in the United States. But it was the longer poem in 1922 that brought him the wider celebrity, including the notice of daily newspapers and popular magazines. His title, "the waste land," entered the public consciousness as a catchphrase that caught the new mood of modernity and the post-Great War period. Looking back to that moment in time, one cannot help but be surprised by the interest which the brainy young American suddenly provoked in Britain. Admittedly this attention was due, at least in part, to the notoriety of the modernist avant-garde with which Eliot was identified. Mainstream society was easily scandalized and the popular media did their part by playing up the antics of artists and writers they considered radical and even dangerous, especially in their influence on public and private morality. But this kind of media-fueled balloon usually deflates as quickly as it is blown up. Someone or something else, more shocking and scandalous, comes along to crowd out the last best thing. The furore moves on; everyday people shake their heads and are deliciously scandalized anew. What is curious and paradoxical about Eliot is that he was able to outlast the fizz of celebrity caused by *The Waste Land* and to see it transformed into a more durable renown.

First of all, as an American, Eliot could not be easily identified as occupying a particular class position within British society. He was in many ways a free agent in a society that was keenly attuned to class and social position as manifested in speech, gesture, and manners. As an obviously intelligent and cultured representative of the New World, he did not fit in and, for once, this was a good thing. In a Britain exhausted by war, death, and the physical and emotional mutilations of battle, Americans in general seemed like saviors, free of the social and political baggage of old Europe. Woodrow Wilson's mission to change the old order in Europe at Versailles had raised the hopes of a battered Continent. America was the promised land of peace, prosperity, and democracy. Eliot, however, was not a Wilsonian idealist; indeed, he was very much opposed to the political optimism coming across the Atlantic from America, He believed that the Wilsonian rhetoric of American-style democracy and the self-determination of peoples rested on a flawed vision of society, an idea that he would develop in his social and cultural criticism over the next four decades. Nevertheless, he enjoyed, along with other trans-planted Americans, the curiosity and respect that attached to the Wilson mission in its early days. That the Wilsonian project ended in failure was put down to the machinations of crafty European statesmen who had no interest in bringing to light a new world rather than to the naïveté and blindness of the President.

To the intellectuals among whom Eliot moved at the time, his more pessimistic diagnosis of the state of the modern world in *The Waste Land* struck a chord the emotional truth of which could not be denied. This is an important point in understanding Eliot's fame. Emotionally, the poem was immediately comprehended, but what it actually said, its meaning, was not that easy to decipher. And that is perhaps the second reason why Eliot's fame extended past the boomlet of general interest that his poem caused. The poem's sibylline utterances, its enigmatic juxtapositions, fragmentary charac-ter, and bewildering range of references, including the evocations of the fertility cults of the ancient Near East and of Asia, harmonized well with an atmosphere of doubt, confusion, and helplessness. Old values and traditions were under attack and, in the vacuum, a literary work like *The Waste Land*, speaking in the tongues of what sounded like visionary or prophetic experi-ence, suggested that Eliot had managed to grasp the problems of a disturbing modernity. That he was able to relate contemporary dilemmas of, say, sexuality, with ancient paradigms seemed doubly impressive. In an age which had lost its confidence, the poem seemed a courageous, perhaps even heroic, confrontation with abject despair.

More impressive still was the fact that it did not describe abjection, but enacted it, so that the reader could experience it internally as a datum of feeling rather than as an aestheticized concept. The poem, moreover, did not offer facile or programmatic solutions for a wounded age, one increasingly suspicious of the glib fix, but suggested that salvation was far off, not easily attained, and attainable only after great sacrifice. Although the poem is often described as a quest narrative, it is more like a pilgrimage, a journey of salvation to the shrine of a mysterious god-figure, or, at a minimum, purga-tion and cleansing of a soiled subjectivity. That this particular pilgrim's progress ended in a confusion of tongues and failure also resonated with the time and added to Eliot's authority as a learned visionary. Triumph did not suit the mood of the time; breakdown, bankruptcy, and obscurity brought readers closer to their own sense of dejection and in this the poem succeeded beyond Eliot's, or anyone's, wildest expectations. It was one of those curious, antiheroic success stories that later become so common in the twentieth century.

Eliot's fame spread from this first achievement in a number of directions. The sibylline character of *The Waste Land* brought Eliot the immediate attention of a new generation of literary critics and scholars in the universities. I. A. Richards, F. R. Leavis, and Helen Gardner in Britain, F. O. Mathiesson, Cleanth Brooks, and others in America found in Eliot the exemplary modern poet, the poet for a new age of doubt, skepticism, and irony. Intense critical examination of Eliot's works has never slackened in the following decades. At first, his poetry was the primary focus, but this soon expanded to take in his literary criticism, his cultural criticism, his personal life, and his activities as a publisher and public figure. With the founding of the *Criterion*, his involvement in the London publishing and editing scene also increased his visibility. More importantly, though, his editorial work for the new journal and his position with Faber and Faber meant that he was one of the central figures in the discovery and encouragement of new writers and new works. In this way, his influence extended well beyond the interest and authority of his own works. Over the years he became one of the most authoritative editorial figures on the scene in one of the most important (if not the most important) publishing centers of the English-speaking world.

The matter of Eliot's declaration of faith in the Church of England in 1927 also brought him attention and to some extent a different kind of notoriety. This time his act of affiliation with the English Establishment scandalized his associates in the modernist avant-garde rather than ordinary society. It has been said that the Church of England is the Establishment at prayer and that a high-profile conversion signifies more than a religious preference, such as one deciding on principle alone to become a Buddhist. Joining the Church of England signaled a wider set of loyalties. That shortly after his conversion Eliot took British citizenship and defined himself as "classicist in literature, royalist in politics and anglo-catholic in religion" (*LA* 15) conveyed to everyone the reach and depth of his new commitments. This movement toward mainstream society did not meet with universal acclaim, though Church leaders were delighted that a prominent poet and cultural figure had taken so radical a step. It was his former avant-garde comrades-in-arms in the European culture wars, however, who were most surprised and, in many cases, disgusted by what they saw as an act of betrayal of the aesthetic and cultural affirmations of their youth. Others in the early 1930s were not sure how to react to Eliot's act of faith. His use of dramatic monologue as a form in his early poetry and the ironic timbre of his work led to speculation that his involvement with the Church was, in some sense, ironic or even a particularly daring piece of high camp.

Nothing could have been further from the truth. Eliot meant what he was saying; he was not exploiting dramatis personae in order to explore, experimentally, unfamiliar areas of feeling. He believed in his Christian avowals in a spirit of orthodoxy that was and, perhaps, still is shockingly foreign to the skeptical tempers of modernity and to the level of intellectual sophistication he had achieved. He believed literally in original sin, hell, and damnation. He believed in the necessity and effectiveness of prayer. He believed in the intercessory powers of the Virgin and in the efficacy of beatitude. For a mind trained to the highest standards of modern philosophy and a poet of the most urbane tastes, an orthodoxy bordering on fundamentalism seemed anomalous. But that was the temper of the man, a strange mixture of sophistication and simplicity. Perhaps this paradox has been elucidated indirectly by Eliot himself in these terms:

> Most people suppose that some people, because they enjoy the luxury of Christian sentiments and the excitement of Christian ritual, swallow or pretend to swallow incredible dogma. For some the process is exactly opposite. Rational assent may arrive late, intellectual conviction may come slowly, but they come inevitably without violence to honesty and nature. To put the sentiments in order is a later and an immensely difficult task: intellectual freedom is earlier and easier than complete spiritual freedom   (*SE* 438)

The division between intellectual and spiritual freedoms is the key to grasping the paradox. The two function, it seems, somewhat independently of each other. Excellence in one requires the utmost in intellectual sophistication; the other requires a radical simplicity, a simplicity that, he will write later, costs no less than everything.

Eliot's religious turn in the late 1920s led to a division of the house, to use a parliamentary metaphor. For some, Eliot's new life was an act of courage that ran against the scientific and materialist grain of modernity. It was an act that invited derision and disappointment. For others, it smacked of an unprincipled sell-out. It was for them the all too familiar story of the former radical making his peace with the Establishment in order to receive the rewards that flow from conformity. The sharp cleavage in esteem ran through Eliot's public career right to the end of his life and has persisted after his death. It has not always been about religion, but the fissure between admiration and scorn has never been bridged or reconciled. On one side of the house, there are those (Hugh Kenner, for example) who believe that Eliot (along with Ezra Pound, James Joyce and Co.) modernized English literature and criticism. They liberated poetry and prose from its Victorian bondage in formal terms and brought to light new experiences, of the modern city for example, or of instability and change as a constant element of existence. Their concentration on language and the self-reflexive aspect of consciousness – the sense that the relationship between words, things, and the mind is not as fixed and staunch as previous generations may have thought – constituted a heroic tale of experiment, innovation, and revival.

Over and against this, the opposition on the other side of the house wove an antithetical narrative in which Eliot's influence takes on a destructive, even sinister, aspect. Of course, the modernists had undertaken a deliberate stratagem of demolition of literary traditions that they believed to be moribund. These older habits of thought and feeling had been inherited from the Romanticism of the nineteenth century and, for many, these traditions still defined the standard by which literary values were assessed. The modernist delight in undermining the foundations of the Romantic past in the name of a new classicism offended those who still believed in the older cultural forms. Moreover, Eliot's cultural and social conservatism, especially after his religious turn, also rankled and, with the passage of time, he was increasingly seen as a regressive force.

But all was not well among the modernists themselves. In America Eliot's detractors saw his embrace of European culture as a betrayal of the new American modernism. His project was seen, from the perspective of a nation beginning to savor its cultural autonomy, as an attempt to keep American culture as a cultural colony of Europe. It was the American modernist poet William Carlos Williams who was most explicit about Eliot's toxicity as a cultural influence. He recorded the effect of *The Waste Land* on his own writing in his *Autobiography*:

> I felt at once that it had set me back twenty years, and I'm sure it did. Critically Eliot returned us to the classroom just at the moment when I felt that we were on the point of an escape to matters much closer to the essence of a new art form itself – rooted in the locality which should give it fruit. I knew at once that in certain ways I was most defeated.[1]

Williams was deeply suspicious of Eliot's Europhilia, seeing it as divorced from the realities of specific times and places. It was airily unhistorical, a magnificent abstraction, possibly, but essentially weightless and bloodless and of little value to the cultural practitioner. If it had any value, it was for the ideological forces of conservatism. In the 1930s this difference of opinion became more intense as the North Atlantic world slipped, firstly, into an economic depression, and then into a social and political crisis that led to the rise of leftist ideologies in direct opposition to right-wing ideas and regimes. Eliot, it was felt, had cast in his lot with the right and was, as a result, suspect in all his words and deeds. That Eliot tried to distance himself from this bipolarity was lost in the din. We must keep in mind that differences of opinion about a writer's work are quite common. What is unique about Eliot is the vehemence of these differences and the way they expanded beyond the work to encompass wider social and political issues.

One of these wider issues was the matter of Eliot's attitude toward Jewish people. The debate about his alleged anti-Semitism began in the 1930s with the publication of *After Strange Gods* in 1934 and it has persisted to our own time. The question of his anti-Semitism is still a regular feature of conferences and journals, and the subject of books, such as Anthony Julius's *T. S. Eliot, Anti-Semitism, and Literary Form* (1995). The issue has been fully debated over the past sixty years, yet it is still unresolved. Was Eliot an anti-Semite? The answer seems to be yes and no at the same time. Yes, he could have been more sensitive to the place of ethnic or cultural minorities in otherwise homogeneous cultures and he could have questioned the anti-Semitic attitudes circulating in England and Europe in the late nineteenth and early twentieth centuries. But, no, he seems not to have hated Jews or to have advocated their persecution and he certainly was not happy about the destruction of European Jewry at the hands of the Nazis during the Second World War. Whether one believes he was an anti-Semite is often entangled with one's attitudes toward other aspects of Eliot's life and work. Many critics and scholars find his religious faith, his poetic theories, and his social and political conservatism offensive regardless of his opinion of Jews. That he may also be an anti-Semite only reinforces and confirms their displeasure. Eliot's admirers and advocates tend to put his statements about Jews in historical contexts that minimize or dilute any purely personal animus. At this distance in time from the 1920s and 1930s, the question of Eliot's anti-Semitism will probably remain forever a point of contention between the two sides of the house.

As Eliot's fame grew, he became very aware of being in the public eye and the controversy about the Jews tarnished the carefully constructed persona of the learned poet, the religious man, and the public personality. He was not happy when the controversy surfaced again in 1947 at an Institute of Contemporary Art poetry reading in London when the Jewish poet Emmanuel

Litvinoff read a poem attacking Eliot's anti-Semitism with Eliot sitting in embarrassed silence in the audience. Others leaped to Eliot's defense but Litvinoff's onslaught was what was reported at length in the newspapers the next day. Eliot survived this awkwardness by letting others defend him; he said and did nothing in response. This was not the case four years later when the young scholar John Peter suggested in an academic article that *The Waste Land* may have homoerotic propensities. Eliot's litigiousness in response exposed a testy side to his personality, now finely tuned to his position as a public intellectual, a man celebrated in the English-speaking world as the greatest of contemporary poets. His resort to the law chilled any scholarly interest in exploring the sexual or erotic dimensions of Eliot's work. It was not until well after his death that the American scholar James E. Miller returned to the homoerotic theme in *The Waste Land* in *T. S. Eliot's Personal Waste Land* (1978). The period of scholarly self-censorship had ended twenty-seven years after the Peter episode.

During the Second World War, Eliot's activities were directed toward war work and especially toward salvaging the European cultural legacy from the general ruin of Europe. It was a rather macabre twist of fate that "the waste land" metaphor for a psychological and emotional state in 1922 was by 1945 literally true. Great swathes of the cities of Europe and of some in England lay in ruins. In the immediate aftermath, Eliot understood that the role of intellectuals in this new situation required calm and composure. After the madness of war and the excessive political rhetoric of the 1930s, something like a traditional wisdom, drawing on the deeper recesses of European culture, was of the utmost necessity. His *Four Quartets* was just such a work, bringing solace to people damaged, physically and emotionally, by the crisis of European civilization. The four poems that make up *Four Quartets* are Eliot's greatest achievements. The poem draws on thirty years of experience as a writer and as a man of letters and might even be considered the greatest poem in English in the twentieth century, a poem that occupies the same cultural place as Tennyson's *In Memoriam, A. H. H.* in the nineteenth century. Like Tennyson's masterpieces, Eliot's is both a personal document, revealing much about his inner life, and a tract for the times. The times were traumatic in a way that surpassed even those following the First World War. *Four Quartets* offered cultural and religious resources by which the traumatized mind might be comforted, and it suggested personal confession as a way of validating the wisdom.

The work's immediate popularity – tens of thousands of copies were sold in the 1940s and it continues to stay in print and find new readers – brought Eliot a new kind of authority. He became a spokesperson for the cultural reconstruction of Europe and spent the years just after the war speaking about the unity of European culture. His was not the only voice in those years, but it was a particularly effective one. Indeed, one could argue that Eliot's efforts helped to lay the foundation for the project of European unity that has led in recent times to the economic and political unification of the Continent, embodied in the institution of the European Union. In these respects, Eliot in the late 1940s and 1950s achieved the status of a public sage. This was the zenith of his reputation as a public figure and for a time it stilled the voices of the opposition. The high point in this period of renown was the awarding of the Nobel Prize for Literature in 1948.

It was in the 1950s that the academic study of Eliot's poetry and prose increased exponentially. The volume of scholarship and critical inquiry has never abated, as any visit to a university or college library can attest. The old debate about the value of Eliot's cultural impact has diminished among scholars as the cultural and political conflicts of the past have receded in time. Instead, scholarship today examines Eliot's body of work from a variety of perspectives without having to take positions of advocacy or attack. This critical interest shows no signs of waning. In recent years new approaches in literary study have turned their focus to Eliot and reevaluated his work in the light of new critical movements and theories. Feminism, structuralism, and poststructuralism, queer studies, new forms of materialist inquiry, Freudian and Lacanian psychoanalytic investigations, and deconstructive methodologies have enriched the critical field and brought Eliot into the twenty-first century as a figure with whom we must still reckon in understanding the evolution of North Atlantic culture.

Notes

1 Life

1. Arthur Symons, *Symbolist Movement in Literature* (London: Heinemann, 1899). Symons was the English critic who was most responsible for the spread of French influence in English letters in the early years of the twentieth century.
2. Bertrand Russell, *Autobiography* 2 vols. (London: Allen and Unwin, 1968), II, p. 150.
3. Conrad Aiken, *U Shant: An Autobiographical Narrative.* (1952; rpt: New York: Meridian books, 1962), p. 258.
4. Carole Seymour-Jones, *Painted Shadow: The Life of Vivienne Eliot* (New York: Doubleday, 2002).
5. T. S. Eliot, "Ulysses, Order, and Myth," *Dial* 75.5 (November 1923), pp. 480–483.
6. Robert Crawford, *The Savage and the City in the Work of T. S. Eliot* (Oxford: Clarendon Press, 1987).
7. Frank Morley, "T. S. Eliot," in Morley, *T. S. Eliot: The Man and His Work* (New York: Delacorte Press, 1966), p. 5.
8. Peter Ackroyd, *T. S. Eliot* (London: Sphere, 1985), p. 319.

2 Contexts

1. In *Inventions of the March Hare, Poems 1909–1917*, ed. Christopher Ricks (San Diego: Harcourt Brace, 1996), pp. 78–79.
2. See the January 1930 number of *Criterion*, p. 5.
3. Lee Oser, *T. S. Eliot and American Poetry* (Columbia: University of Missouri Press, 1998), pp. 104–125.

3 Works

1. Robert Crawford, *The Savage and the City in the Work of T. S. Eliot* (Oxford: Clarendon Press, 1987).
2. Martin Heidegger, *An Introduction to Metaphysics*, trans. Ralph Mannheim (Garden City: Anchor Books, 1961), p. 42.

3. Lyndall Gordon, *Eliot's Early Years* (Oxford: Oxford University Press, 1977), p. 14. Further quotations will be cited parenthetically in the text.
4. Peter Gay, *The Bourgeois Experience: Victoria to Freud, Volume I: Education of the Senses* (New York: Oxford University Press, 1984), p. 329.
5. When asked in later life how he came up with the name Prufrock for the poem, Eliot could not remember. The name, however, dates back to the St. Louis of his youth, where advertisements for a furniture wholesaler named Prufrock-Littau appeared in the local press in the first decade of the twentieth century.
6. Arthur Hugh Clough, *The Poems*, ed. A. L. P. Norrington (London: Oxford University Press, 1968), Canto II, ll. 292–295, p. 196.
7. Robert Langbaum, *The Poetry of Experience: The Dramatic Monologue in Modern Literary Tradition* (New York: W. W. Norton, 1957), p. 85.
8. Julia Kristeva, *Powers of Horror: An Essay on Abjection*, trans. Léon S. Roudiez (New York: Columbia University Press, 1982). Further quotations will be cited parenthetically in the text.
9. Lytton Strachey, *Eminent Victorians* (1918; rpt. Harmondsworth: Penguin Books, 1971), pp. 9–11.
10. Hugh Kenner, *The Invisible Poet: T. S. Eliot* (London: Methuen, 1966), pp. 6–7.
11. Michael Edwards, *Eliot/Language* (Breakish: Aquila Publishing, 1975), p. 11.
12. Percy Bysshe Shelley, *The Complete Poetical Works*, ed. Thomas Hutchison (London: Oxford University Press, 1960), p. 673.
13. Jessie L. Weston, *From Ritual to Romance* (Garden City: Doubleday Anchor Books, 1957).
14. Leon Surette, *The Birth of Modernism: Ezra Pound, T. S. Eliot, W. B. Yeats and the Occult* (Montreal: McGill-Queen's University Press, 1993).
15. Rupert Brooke, *The Poetical Works*, ed. Geoffrey Keynes (London: Faber and Faber, 1970), p. 174.
16. Evelyn Waugh, *Brideshead Revisited* (1945; rpt. Harmondsworth: Penguin Books, 1983), p. 42.
17. Guido Cavalcanti was a contemporary of Dante and part of a wide circle of Italian writers in the thirteenth century known as the *trecentisti*. The line adapted by Eliot is from a poet by Cavalcanti translated into English by Dante Gabriel Rossetti as "Ballata, written in Exile at Sarzana."
18. Henry Vaughan, *The Complete Poetry*, ed. French Fogle (New York: W. W. Norton, 1964), ll. 1–2, p. 231.
19. John Donne, *The Complete Poetry*, ed. John T. Shawcross (Garden City: Anchor Books, 1967), l. 1, p. 344.
20. Richard Crashaw, *The Complete Poetry*, ed. George Walton Williams (Garden City: Anchor Books, 1970), ll. 1–2, p. 371.
21. Keith Alldritt, *Eliot's Four Quartets: Poetry as Chamber Music* (London: The Woburn Press, 1978), pp. 37–40.
22. Kathleen Freeman, *Ancilla to the Pre-Socratic Philosophers* (Oxford: Basil Blackwell, 1956), pp. 24–25.

23. Ibid., p. 29.
24. Karl Barth, *The Epistle to the Romans*, trans, Edwyn C. Hoskins (London: Oxford University Press, 1968), p. 46.
25. Ibid.
26. Frank Kermode, *The Sense of an Ending* (New York: Oxford University Press), p. 49.

4 Critical reception

1. William Carlos Williams, *Autobiography* (New York: New Directions, 1971), p. 174.

The works of T. S. Eliot

After Strange Gods: A Primer of Modern Heresy. London: Faber and Faber, 1934.

Collected Plays. London: Faber and Faber, 1968.

Collected Poems: 1909–1962 (CP). London: Faber and Faber, 1968.

For Lancelot Andrewes: Essays on Style and Order. London: Faber and Faber, 1928.

The Idea of a Christian Society. London: Faber and Faber, 1939.

Inventions of the March Hare: Poems 1909–1917. Ed. Christopher Ricks.
        San Diego: Harcourt Brace, 1996.

Letters. Ed. Valerie Eliot. San Diego: Harcourt Brace Jovanovich, 1988.

Notes Towards the Definition of Culture. 1948; rpt. London: Faber and Faber, 1988.

Old Possum's Book of Practical Cats. London: Faber and Faber, 1950.

On Poetry and Poets. London: Faber and Faber, 1957.

The Sacred Wood: Essays on Poetry and Criticism. 1919; rpt. London: Methuen,
        1957.

Selected Essays. 1932; rpt. London: Faber and Faber, 1951.

To Criticize the Critic, and Other Writings. New York: Farrar, Straus and Giroux,
        1965.

The Use of Poetry and the Use of Criticism. 1933; rpt. London: Faber and Faber,
        1964.

Further reading

Ackroyd, Peter. *T. S. Eliot.* London: Hamilton, 1984. An objective and penetrating biography of the poet.

Alldritt, Keith. *Eliot's Four Quartets: Poetry as Chamber Music.* London: Woburn Press, 1978. Examines Eliot's use of sonata form in the composition of *Four Quartets.*

Asher, Kenneth George. *T. S. Eliot and Ideology.* Cambridge: Cambridge University Press, 1995. A thorough and incisive account of the background to Eliot's social and cultural criticism.

Bedient, Calvin. *He Do the Police in Different Voices: The Waste Land and its Protagonist.* Chicago: University of Chicago Press, 1986. A detailed study of the voices in the poem, with an emphasis on the role of Tiresias.

Brooker, Jewel Spears. *Mastery and Escape: T. S. Eliot and the Dialectic of Modernism.* Amherst: University of Massachusetts Press, 1994. An excellent analysis of Eliot's relationship to literary modernism.
ed. *T. S. Eliot: The Contemporary Reviews.* Cambridge: Cambridge University Press, 2004. An indispensable guide to Eliot's reception among his contemporaries.

Bush, Ronald. *T. S. Eliot: A Study in Character and Style.* New York: Oxford University Press, 1983. An intelligent and sensitive study of Eliot's style and its relation to his psychology.
T. S. Eliot: The Modernist in History. Cambridge: Cambridge University Press, 1991. A series of essays on Eliot and concepts of history.

Childs, Donald J. *T. S. Eliot: Mystic, Son and Lover.* London: Athlone Press, 1997. An important critical work on Eliot's belief system.

Chinitz, David E. *T. S. Eliot and the Cultural Divide.* Chicago: University of Chicago Press, 2003. A groundbreaking account of Eliot's interest in and use of popular culture in America and England.

Cowan, Laura, Sebastian David Guy Knowles, and Scott A. Leonard, eds. *T. S. Eliot: Man and Poet.* Orono, ME: National Poetry Foundation, 1990. A wide variety of critical and biographical essays with much useful information.

Crawford, Robert. *The Savage and the City in the Work of T. S. Eliot.* Oxford: Clarendon Press, 1987. A very stimulating analysis of a central paradox in Eliot's poetry.

Cuddy, Lois A. *T. S. Eliot and the Poetics of Evolution: Sub/Versions of Classicism, Culture and Progress.* Lewisburg: Bucknell University Press, 2000. Provocative readings of Eliot's major works, with a poststructuralist bent.

Davidson, Hamet, ed. *T. S. Eliot.* London and New York: Longman, 1999. Important essays excerpted from works by the leading critics in Eliot studies.

Dawson, J. L., P. D. Holland, and D. J. McKitterick. *A Concordance to the Complete Poems and Plays of T. S. Eliot.* Ithaca: Cornell University Press, 1995. A very useful tool for advanced work on Eliot's texts.

Donoghue, Denis. *Words Alone: The Poet, T. S. Eliot.* New Haven: Yale University Press, 2000. A very accessible engagement with Eliot's language.

Frye, Northrop. *T. S. Eliot.* Edinburgh: Oliver and Boyd, 1964. A somewhat jaundiced but fair introduction to Eliot's ideas and works.

Gardner, Helen. *The Art of T. S. Eliot.* New York: Dutton, 1950. An early but still very useful analysis of Eliot's mastery of literary form, especially in *Four Quartets.*

Gordon, Lyndall. *T. S. Eliot: An Imperfect Life.* New York: Norton, 1999. The most recent biography of Eliot with much new material.

Habib, Rafey. *The Early T. S. Eliot and Western Philosophy.* Cambridge: Cambridge University Press, 1999. An excellent account of Eliot's philosophical reading and the background to his early thought.

Jain, Manju. *T. S. Eliot and American Philosophy: The Harvard Years.* Cambridge: Cambridge University Press, 1992. The best account of Eliot's early engagements with philosophy at Harvard University.

Julius, Anthony. *T. S. Eliot, Anti-Semitism and Literary Form.* Cambridge: Cambridge University Press, 1995. A prosecutorial attack on Eliot's attitudes toward Jews and the impact on his poetry.

Kearns, Cleo McNelly. *T. S. Eliot and Indic Traditions: A Study in Poetry and Belief.* Cambridge: Cambridge University Press, 1987. An important study of Eliot's exposure to and use of Indian religious traditions.

Kenner, Hugh. *The Invisible Poet: T. S. Eliot.* London: Methuen, 1966. Still one of the very best critical works on Eliot both in explaining his poetics of impersonality and in its relevance to a reading of his works.

Laity, Cassandra, and Nancy K. Gish, eds. *Gender, Desire and Sexuality in T. S. Eliot.* Cambridge: Cambridge University Press, 2004. Thought-provoking engagements with Eliot's texts from a number of theoretical perspectives.

Manganiello, Dominic. *T. S. Eliot and Dante.* Basingstoke: Macmillan Press, 1989. Examines the influence of Dante on Eliot and Eliot's interpretations of the Italian poet.

Menand, Louis. *Discovering Modernism: T. S. Eliot and his Context.* New York: Oxford University Press, 1988. An important contextual study of Eliot, especially his relation to the modernist movement.

Miller, James E. *T. S. Eliot's Personal Waste Land: Exorcism of the Demons.* University Park: Pennsylvania State University Press, 1978. A pioneering study of *The Waste Land* as possibly homoerotic in subtext.

Moody, A. D. *Thomas Stearns Eliot, Poet.* Cambridge: Cambridge University Press, 1979. Good readings of major poems with reference to sources and literary history.
   The Cambridge Companion to T. S. Eliot. Cambridge: Cambridge University Press, 1994. Essays surveying the life, work, and legacy of the poet.

Oser, Lee. *T. S. Eliot and American Poetry.* Columbia: University of Missouri Press, 1998. A useful if somewhat exaggerated study, placing of Eliot in relation to the American philosopher Ralph Waldo Emerson and American literary history.

Perl, Jeffrey M. *Skepticism and Modern Enmity: Before and After Eliot.* Baltimore: Johns Hopkins University Press, 1989. An excellent examination of Eliot's place in modern philosophical traditions and in the cultural history of modernity.

Raine, Craig. *In Defence of T. S. Eliot.* London: Picador, 2000. An interesting defense of Eliot against recent attacks on his reputation by a fellow poet and one of Eliot's successors as poetry editor at Faber and Faber.

Ricks, Christopher. *T. S. Eliot and Prejudice.* London: Faber and Faber, 1988. A defense of Eliot written at a time when the poet was under attack for anti-Semitism.

Riquelme, John Paul. *Harmony of Dissonances: T. S. Eliot, Romanticism, and Imagination.* Baltimore: Johns Hopkins University Press, 1991. A stimulating account of Eliot's poetics and his ambiguous relationship to the romantic tradition.

Sigg, Eric. *The American T. S. Eliot: A Study of the Early Writings.* Cambridge: Cambridge University Press, 1989. Emphasizes Eliot's American roots and examines his early poetry in that context.

Smith, Grover. *T. S. Eliot's Poetry and Plays: A Study in Sources and Meaning.* Chicago: University of Chicago Press, 1974. Still the best study of the literary and historical sources of Eliot's poetry and plays.
   T. S. Eliot and the Use of Memory. London: Associated University Presses, 1996. An accessible account of an important dimension of Eliot's poetry.

Southam, B. C. *A Student's Guide to the Selected Poems of T. S. Eliot.* London: Faber and Faber, 1994. Originally published in 1969, this small book offers elementary, but informed, readings of Eliot's major poems.

Thormählen, Marianne. *The Waste Land: A Fragmentary Wholeness.* Lund: LiberLäromedel/Gleerup, 1978. A detailed account of the problems involved in establishing the unity of *The Waste Land.*

Williamson, George. *A Reader's Guide to T. S. Eliot: A Poem-by-Poem Analysis.* New York: Noonday Press, 1966. Still useful as a study of sources, though a little outdated in its readings of the poetry.

Index

Verdenal, Jean 4
Vidler, Alec 92
Vienna 69
Vittoz, Roger 11, 26, 63, 79
Vorticism 25

Wagner, Richard 67, 69, 71
Waste Land, The 5, 8, 9, 10–12,
    16, 26, 27, 30, 36, 43, 51,
    52, 55, 59, 61, 62–79, 81, 84,
    86, 93, 107, 108, 109, 110, 115
Waugh, Evelyn 79, 84
Weaver, Harriet Shaw 7

Westminster Abbey 21
Weston, Jessie L. 64–5, 69
"What is a Classic?" 93, 94
Whibley, Charles 12
Williams, William Carlos 113
Wilson, Woodrow 109
Woods, J. H. 28
Woolf, Leonard and Virginia 8, 12
World Council of Churches 91
Wordsworth, William 94
Wyndham, George 49

Yeats, W. B. 100, 101